TWAYNE'S WORLD AUTHORS SERIES

A Survey of the World's Literature

Sylvia E. Bowman, Indiana University

GENERAL EDITOR

GERMANY

Professor Ulrich Weisstein
Indiana University, Bloomington

EDITOR

Ernst Jünger

TWAS 323

Photograph courtesy of Pressebildarchiv Heinz Finke

Ernst Jünger

Ernst Jünger

By GERHARD LOOSE

Professor Emeritus, University of Rochester

Twayne Publishers, Inc.   ::   New York

Library of Congress Cataloging in Publication Data

Loose, Gerhard, 1907-
    Ernst Jünger.

    (Twayne's world authors series, TWAS 323. Germany)
    Bibliography: p. 133.
    1. Jünger, Ernst, 1895- .
PT2619.U43Z659   838'.9'1209   74-4150
ISBN 0-8057-2479-6

MANUFACTURED IN THE UNITED STATES OF AMERICA

For
Monica and Bronwyn

Acknowledgments

The passages from *On the Marble Cliffs* by Ernst Jünger, translated by Stuart Hood, copyright 1970, are reprinted with the permission of Penguin Books Ltd., Middlesex, Harmondsworth, England.

All other works of Ernst Jünger quoted within this book, including *Der Friede* (The Peace) and *Glaserne Bienen* (Glass Bees) which are now out of print, are reprinted with the permission of Ernst Klett Verlag, Stuttgart, Germany.

Passages quoted from *The Doors of Perception* by Aldous Huxley, copyright 1970, are reprinted with the permission Harper and Row, Publishers, Inc., New York.

Contents

About the Author

Gerhard Loose was born and educated in Germany. He studied at the Universities of Leipzig and Vienna, receiving the Ph.D. degree in 1933. A voluntary exile from Nazi Germany, he came to the United States in 1934. He held positions at the Riverdale Country School in New York City, Haverford College, Lafayette College, the Universities of Colorado and Rochester. As visiting lecturer, he served at the City College of New York, Vassar College, the University of California at Berkeley, Purdue University and the University of Texas.

In 1942, Mr. Loose enlisted in the United States Army, rising from private to captain. He served in the European Theater of Operations.

His fields of scholarly interest are modern German literature and comparative literature. His books include *Ernst Jünger, Gestalt und Werk, Die Ästhetik Gottfried Benns* and *Franz Kafka und Amerika.* He also published some thirty articles and ninety reviews. His reasearch has been supported by the American Council of Learned Societies, the John Simon Guggenheim Memorial Foundation and four faculty fellowships.

In 1969, Dr. Loose retired from teaching. He now lives in Danby, Vermont, devoting his time to writing.

Preface

Ernst Jünger, whose literary career spans some fifty years, is probably the most controversial German writer of our time. He fits no conventional category, nor can he be identified with any one movement or school. More important, it is the protean nature of his thought and work that is the bane of the critic. So, with equal force and temper, he has been praised and denigrated, glorified and condemned, raised to a pedestal and denied any legitimate accomplishment.

The range of Jünger's concerns is wide, and they are apparently disparate. He is a man of action (soldier, politician), yet equally inclined to the contemplative life. Although he extols war, he also seeks to contribute to peace. His posture is that of the radical nationalist *and* the cosmopolitan, the revolutionary *and* the conservative. The humanistic tradition is both rejected and reaffirmed by him. He is at home in his native land and, inveterate traveler that he is, equally so on the several continents. Curious yet easeful, he moves in society only to return to rustic seclusion. Unflinchingly he confronts nihilism, convinced that life, in all its aspects, is meaningful. In an irreligious age, he seeks to reaffirm faith and belief. As a student of history, he insists on the verities of the myth. The machine fascinates him but plant and animal arouse equal, and even greater, curiosity. One of his enduring and scientifically productive interests is biology, notably the study of insects which, however, does not hamper but rather sustains his search for metaphysical truth. The world of the psyche is consciously explored and darkly experienced by him in dreams and by dint of drug-induced visions.

How, then, may the paradox be dissolved, the contradictions reconciled, the conflicts resolved? The discords fuse into harmony if Ernst Jünger is seen as what he is essentially: *homo ludens*, man at play. The term is Huizinga's, who has shown that play is a constituent element of every culture. manifestations of which are encountered in such fundamental and diverse concerns as war and art, law and knowledge. A few examples may help indicate what is involved here. Basically, at least in most instances, play is tantamount to contest. A legal dispute, however bitterly contested, has the earmarks of a game: the court is the playground; rules, both procedural and legal, apply; plaintiff and defendant, judge and counsel play clearly defined parts. I do not, of course, mean to say that adversary proceedings such as these are merely a game; however, the element of play inheres in them. In the Middle Ages, the so-called ordeal also assumed the form of a combative contest. If the accused prevailed, he had proved his innocence; if he was defeated, he was pronounced guilty. This type of ordeal is reminiscent of the joust, in which two knights prove their fighting skill. War, serious matter that it is, may also be "played." The proficiency of an army, particularly the skill of the officers, is tested in "war games." And children, *lusori par excellence*, "play war" with appropriate toys or among themselves.

The riddle is a game involving knowledge. It plays a part in the myth (Oedipus answers the question posed by the Sphinx) and the fairy tale (the princess testing her suitors), but it is also designed as a game for the individual alone (crossword puzzles and the like; "quiz programs" on radio and television are also cases in point). The sophist is the man who plays with ideas; his argumentation may indeed strike us as *ludi*crous.

The arts provide a key of understanding outright what is meant by play. The musician "plays" a composition. A literary work written for stage performance is called a "play," its author a "playwright." There is even the play within the play (*Hamlet, i. a.*). The drama may be characterized as a serious contest, which, in comedy, is of the playful kind. Within the literary work, word and syntax, that is, style, may be the object of play. In this respect, Thomas Mann is eminently *homo ludens*.

From observing the element of play in various human endeavors, we turn to the general, basic question: what is play? It is an activity that is essentially social or socializing, although there are games, like solitaire, which do not require a partner. Play is an activity that is either physical (football) or mental (chess). It is freely engaged in; where a person participates in it against his will, its spirit is violated, for a disinclined player is a sorry sight, a pathetic figure.

Play does not accomplish anything. One plays for the sake of playing. This idea may, of course, be subverted by the "professional" for whom playing is a way of making money — primarily, but not exclusively. Although he produces nothing tangible or useful, *homo ludens* is very serious in what he does. He who plays at playing mocks the game, treats the rules in a cavalier fashion, or cheats just for the fun of it, is a "Spielverderber," one who spoils the game and kills the joy of it. This is the paradox of play: the more seriously one is involved, the more pleasure he derives from it.

I have said that play accomplishes nothing. It is a test of skill — physical, mental, or both. Although the successful player enjoys his superiority, a game well played but lost is also a source of pleasure. By contrast, being a "bad loser" is opprobrious. The joy of playing may be, and often is, a vicarious experience. Watching others at play is pleasurable.

Both participant and spectator seek and find release — from the ordinary and commonplace, from work and drudgery, duty and obligation, i.e., from the whole "system of constructive purposes." Much leisure time is spent playing — playing as hard as one works, or even harder. The day's labor may be exhausting, but energies that seek release "after hours" are still left.

Play, as I have said, is serious business. It is imperative that the rules be strictly observed but also that the game be played energetically, to the full extent of the participant's resources. Only if this is done do the aesthetic elements or aspects of play, such as rhythm and harmony, become manifest. This is the measure of perfection which elicits the admiring comment "beautifully played."

Most human activities are engaged in within society. But they are not only socially but also morally relevant because what we do, and the way we do it, affects others, positively or negatively, helps or hinders, enriches or exploits them, and augments or diminishes their well-being. Play, however, is amoral because it neither gives nor takes away. Only the Puritan objects; for in his eyes, any activity that is not directed toward a "serious," materially or spiritually constructive end, is immoral.

There are distinct species of *homo ludens*; the adventurer ranges among them. For him, life is play, a game. Risk, even danger, is his element. The outcome of an adventure is always uncertain; but suspense is what he seeks and wherein he revels. He is a restless kind of man because the quest of the venturesome undertaking never ends. He has an excess of vital energy. He acts, must act, to discharge it. Not seeking to accomplish anything tangible or constructive, he is content with satisfying his ego. He may, of course, amass wealth or make a beneficial discovery, but this is incidental, adventitious, not the true object of his activity. It is the unknown, the *terra incognita* of the physical world as well as the realm of mind and psyche, that is his habitat and sphere of action. The adventurer is, ideally speaking, an extreme individualist, whose game is — metaphorically — "solitaire."

Ernst Jünger's life and work can only be understood *sub specie ludi*: the lack of enduring commitment, the sudden and frequent changes of posture, the rich and seemingly inexhaustible variety of his concerns, all point to a man at play. Although self-characterizations are not necessarily binding, it is significant that Jünger, in a rare moment of candor, spoke of himself as "homo ludens." And it is equally significant that he did so late in his career, when this view of himself extended over more than sixty years. (*Zwei Inseln: Formosa, Ceylon,* p. 44.)

The playground is vast; it is the world: the continents, the realms of plant and animal, and man, the individual and the social being. Action and contemplation are equal sources of gratification. Variety and variation are the characteristics — in sharp contrast to the single-minded, obsessive concern of a man like Bobby Fischer.

Travel that does not pursue a rationally conceived and justified goal such as discovery or business but is prompted by the excitement and pleasure it affords may properly be called play. Already as a boy, Jünger began to seek the world in this manner. He joined the *Wandervögel* (German youth movement), who — as the name suggests — explored the land hiking and camping. The adolescent ran away from home and enlisted in the French Foreign Legion, but only reached Algeria. Once there, he intended to desert, to strike out for that part of the continent that was yet dark and mysterious. Growing older, he used the conventional means of locomotion. He has sailed the seven seas, missing only — so far — Australasia. What he saw and found to his pleasure has been recorded in numerous travel diaries.

The world of plant and animal also arouses Jünger's playful curiosity. He is a skillful gardener and a competent botanist. Entomology, a lifelong hobby of his, has gained him professional recognition but, more important, afforded him the pleasures of the hunter, a species of *homo ludens*. He calls his entomological pursuits either "Insektenbelustigungen" (entertainment with insects) or "subtile Jagden" (a chase employing subtle means, affording delicate pleasures).

In the world of man, Jünger's activities have been extensive and unusually diverse. For no less than fifteen years he was a military man, serving in both world wars and the *Reichswehr*, the army of the Weimar Republic. In 1914, the young patriot enlisted to serve his country. But war also meant something else for him. As his brother Friedrich Georg states: "War may also be considered a game of chance. And it has always been considered as such. Just as the gambler knows that chance is of the essence, so, too, does the man who eagerly goes out to fight a war. Both are adventurers." Particularly in World War I, Jünger sought adventure and found it. But he also sought what modern warfare with its employment of masses of matériel and men denied him: the kind of combat which pits two individuals against each other, the contest which measures skill and valor according to chivalric rules. War as a game, such as the knights had fought it, was no longer possible.

After returning to civilian life and a brief academic interlude, Jünger involved himself in politics, which, for him, was but another kind of agonistic activity. As a revolutionary nationalist, he fought against capitalist democracy, his weapon being the pen. He engaged in the game of radical ideas, never fearful of where the logic of uncompromising search would lead him. It culminated in *Der Arbeiter* (1932), an exposition of militant totalitarianism. He seemed to be committed, but was not. It had merely been his pleasure to play a part in the arena of politics. The game was over when this kind of venturesome curiosity was stilled; and when after 1933 totalitarian politics became the order of the day, he withdrew, bored and disgusted. Daringly, he engaged the powers that be in *Auf den Marmorklippen*, a thinly veiled allegorical novel in which he rises *in tyrannis*.

In creating the machine, *homo faber* — the very opposite of *homo ludens* — has demonstrated incomparable ingenuity and skill. Jünger explores its twofold potential, its constructive as well as destructive use. *Heliopolis*, a novel projected into the distant future, contains elements of science fiction created by the playful imagination. In *Gläserne Bienen*, a fictionalized *homo ludens* puts the automaton to his use.

Jünger is a gregarious person. Of this capacity he gives the best account, and paradoxically so, in *Strahlungen*, his diary of World War II. For more than three years he was stationed in Paris, serving in the staff of the German high command in occupied France. In this particular circle, his contacts with numerous and diverse personalities, including the commanding general, were social as well as professional and, indeed, political; and thus he came to know some of the leading figures involved in the conspiracy against Hitler. Parisian society, an odd playground in times of war, was open to him. He met Vichy politicians, American expatriates, writers such as Céline and Marcel Jouhandeau, and Braque and Picasso from among the artists. The diary shows that he made full use of the opportunity to play the social game. It proves his claim that, for the writer, there is no such thing as bad company.

Although Jünger is very much a man of the present, his perspective is wide. His imagination plays upon the past, a favorite object of his speculations being the myth. Equally fascinated by the future event, he displays an almost boundless curiosity about the things to come, allowing his speculations full play in the political essay (*An der Zeitmauer*) as well as in the novel.

Man is a social being, but he is also an individual endowed with a psyche incomparably his own. Jünger's particular concern is the dark recesses of the soul into which he makes venturesome forays. *Das abenteuerliche Herz* records his findings. Typical are the numerous descriptions of his dreams and dreamlike experiences. Throughout his life, he has been playing upon his psyche by ingesting drugs, including those of parlous potency, long before it became a fashion. *Annäherungen* fully describes these psychic ventures.

Jünger may also be characterized as a scientist in quest of quintessential truth, or as a rationalist in pursuit of the metaphysical verities. The established fact serves as the point of departure for the unrestricted play of his speculative powers. The search for ultimate truth also encompasses religion. Jünger is not a believer but, on occasion, he has shown the need to be one. It is characteristic of him that recognizing, accepting a supreme being can only result from an agonistic contest in which he and the divine engage each other.

Homo ludens is the *Leitfigur* of Ernst Jünger's life and work. It provides the guidance through what may appear to be a maze of contradictions and paradoxes.

GERHARD LOOSE

Danby, Vermont

Chronology

1895   Born on March 29 in Heidelberg. One of his brothers, Friedrich Georg, will also become a well-known man of letters. Father: Ernst Georg J., chemist and apothecary; mother: Karoline Lample J.

1913   Runs away from home to join the French Foreign Legion. Being a minor, he is discharged at his father's request.

1914   Graduates from high school. Enlists in the army. Serves on the Western front for the duration of the war.

1916   Commissioned as second lieutenant in the infantry. Company commander.

1918   Wounded in action for the seventh time. Awarded the "Pour le mérite," the highest distinction for valor.

1919-   Officer in the *Reichswehr.*
1923

1920   *In Stahlgewittern* (World War I diary in novelistic form), his first and most widely read book.

1922   *Der Kampf als inneres Erlebnis* (essay on the psychology of combat).

1923-   Studies biology in Leipzig and Naples.
1926

1923   *Sturm* (short novel about an attack on the Western front).

1924   *Feuer und Blut* (narrative about the offensive on the Somme river in March, 1917).

1925-   Contributes to, and edits, radically right-wing journals such
1931   as *Standarte, Arminius, Widerstand,* and *Der Vormarsch.* Contributes to, and edits, compilations concerning various aspects of World War I *(Die Unvergessenen, Der Kampf um das Reich, Das Antlitz des Weltkrieges,* and *Krieg und Krieger).*

1925   Married to Gretha von Jeinsen. *Das Wäldchen 125* (narrative on positional warfare).

1927- Lives in Berlin. Beginning of a career as independent writer.
1933
1927 France: the first of numerous journeys in Europe, to Africa, the Americas, and Asia.
1929 *Das abenteuerliche Herz* (collection of essays).
1931 *Die totale Mobilmachung* (essay on mobilizing for total war).
1932 *Der Arbeiter* (comprehensive exposition of "heroic realism," totalitarian nihilism, and the imminence of the global conflict).
1933 Rejects the offer of the Nationalsozialistische Deutsche Arbeiterpartei (NSDAP) of a seat in the Reichstag. Refuses to join the nazified Deutsche Akademie der Dichtung. Disengagement from politics: "Innere Emigration."
1933- Lives in Goslar. Intensive entomological studies, a field in
1936 which he gains professional status.
1934 *Blätter und Steine* (collection of essays).
1936- Lives in Überlingen on Lake Constance.
1939
1936 *Afrikanische Spiele* (novel about his venture in the French Foreign Legion).
1938 *Das abenteuerliche Herz* (second version).
1939- Lives in Kirchhorst (near Hannover).
1948
1939 *Auf den Marmorklippen* (an allegorical novel *in tyrannis*).
1939- Serves in World War II: duty at the Westwall, with the occu-
1944 pation forces in France, and the supreme command in Paris. Contact with the military planning the assassination of Hitler and the overthrow of the regime.
1942 *Gärten und Strassen* (Part One of the World War II diary). The Nazi regime virtually forbids further publication of his books.
1943 *Myrdun* (on Norway).
1944 Discharged from military service. Ernst, his eldest son, killed in action in Italy.
1945 *Der Friede* (proposal for a postwar global reorganization).
1945- Forbidden to publish in Germany for refusing to submit to
1949 denazification procedures.
1947 *Atlantische Fahrt* (on Brazil, the Canary Islands, Morocco). *Sprache und Körperbau* (essay on the symbolism of language).

1948   *Ein Inselfrühling* (on Sicily and Rhodes).

1948-   Lives in Ravensburg (Württemberg). Experimentation with
1950   drugs such as mescaline and psylocibin.

1949   *Strahlungen* (Part Two of the World War II diary). *Helio-
        polis* (novel).

1950   Lives in Wilflingen (Württemberg).

1950   *Über die Linie* (essay on the overcoming of nihilism).

1951   *Der Waldgang* (essay on the existentialist position).

1952   *Besuch auf Godenholm* (short novel, reflecting the author's
        experimentation with drugs).

1953   *Der gordische Knoten* (essay on the relationship of Orient
        and Occident).

1954   First of nine voyages to Sardinia. *Das Sanduhrbuch* (essay
        on time).

1955   *Am Sarazenenturm* (on Sardinia). Awarded the literary prize
        of the city of Bremen.

1956   Journey to Tuscany. *Rivarol* (translation of R.'s maxims).

1957   *San Pietro* and *Serpentara* (on Sardinia). *Gläserne Bienen*
        (novel).

1958   Voyage to the United States. *Jahre der Okkupation* (postwar
        diary).

1959   Voyage to Greece. Awarded the Grosse Bundesver-
        dienstkreuz. Cofounder and coeditor of the journal *Antaios*.
        An der Zeitmauer (essay on the evolvement of a new age).

1960   Death of Gretha Jünger. *Der Weltstaat* (essay on global
        organization). *Sgraffiti* (essays; sequel to *Das abenteuerliche
        Herz*).

1961   Voyage to Syria, Jordan, and Lebanon.

1962   Married to Liselotte Lohrer. *Das spanische Mondhorn*
        (metaphysical essay anent *Copris hispanus*). Voyage to
        Egypt, the Sudan, and the Sinai.

1963   *Typus, Name, Gestalt* (philosophical essay).

1964   Voyages to Greece and Spitsbergen.

1965   Publication of *Werke* (ten volumes) completed. Awarded the
        Immermann Prize of the City of Düsseldorf. Voyage to East
        Asia.

1966   Voyages to Corsica and Angola. *Grenzgänge* (essays).

1967   Entomological excursion in the Pyrenees. *Subtile Jagden*
        (essays). *Im Granit* (on Corsica).

1968   Voyage to Iceland. *Zwei Inseln* (on Formosa and Ceylon).

1969 Voyages to Piedmont and Morocco.
1970 *Lettern und Ideogramme* (on Japan). *Annäherungen: Drogen und Rausch* (extensive essay on drugs).
1973 *Die Zwille* (novel).

Abbreviations

Wherever possible, the quotations from Jünger's writings were taken from *Werke* (ten volumes, 1960 - 1965). A reference such as AF, 4, 169 indicates: *Atlantische Fahrt,* vol. 4, p. 169. The quotations from books published after 1965 refer to the original editions.

The translations are mine. The exceptions are *Auf den Marmorklippen, Der Friede,* and *Gläserne Bienen:* in these cases I quote from the published translations, though changes have been made to improve the reading.

For full bibliographical information, see the Bibliography.

AF	*Atlantische Fahrt* (1947)
AH(1)	*Das abenteuerliche Herz* (1929) (first version)
AH(2)	*Das abenteuerliche Herz* (1938) (second version)
AM	*On the Marble Cliffs (Auf den Marmorklippen).* tr. Stuart Hood. Harmondsworth, Middlesex: Penguin Books, 1970
Ann	*Annäherungen* (1970)
Ant	*Ein Vormittag in Antibes* (1960)
AS	*Afrikanische Spiele* (1936)
DA	*Der Arbeiter* (1932)
DF	*The Peace (Der Friede).* tr. Stuart Hood. Hinsdale (Ill.): Henry Regnery Company, 1948
FB	*Feuer und Blut* (1925)
GB	*The Glass Bees (Gläserne Bienen).* tr. Louise Brogan and Elizabeth Mayer. New York: The Noonday Press (Farrar, Straus and Cudahy), 1960
GM	*Aus der Goldenen Muschel* (1948)
H	*Heliopolis* (1965) (revised edition; *Werke,* vol 10)
Hel	*Heliopolis* (1949)
IF	*Ein Inselfrühling* (1948)
K	*Der Kampf als inneres Erlebnis* (1922)

LI	*Lettern und Ideogramme* (1970)
Myr	*Myrdun* (1943)
Sat	*Am Sarazenenturm* (1955)
SK	*Sprache und Körperbau* (1947)
SP	*San Pietro* (1957)
Str*	*Strahlungen* (1949)
Str	*Strahlungen* (1955) (revised edition)
W	*Das Wäldchen 125* (1925)
Z	*An der Zeitmauer* (1959)
Zw	*Die Zwille* (1973)

CHAPTER 1

The First World War

ERNST Jünger was born on March 29, 1895, in Heidelberg. His father, who held a doctoral degree in chemistry, was a pharmacist. Although a thoroughly educated man, he inclined to the sciences, less so to the humanities. His wife was also intellectually alive, versed in literature, and truly interested in the emancipation of women. Their son, Ernst, was to become, quite fittingly, a scientist, a man of letters, and a student of public affairs. Although he was a gifted and inquisitive child, he was a poor student. Since his parents moved a great deal, he had to change schools frequently. But what actually accounted for his poor performance was his dislike for the educational methods, the emphasis on form rather than substance, on discipline rather than the free and full development of the child's faculties. As Ernst grew older, this dislike deepened to a hostility toward what is now called the Establishment: an order which considered material gain, social prestige, and security paramount. This opposition was shared by others of his age. At the turn of the century, the *Wandervögel,* a gathering of alienated middle-class youth who escaped from city to country, from civilization to nature, from complex artificiality to frugal naturalness, was founded. These youths banded together in small groups trying to recapture a past which appeared to them simple, colorful, and filled with meaning. Together, they read, engaged in probing discussions, sang the rediscovered folk songs, and spent weekends and vacations on hikes. Jünger joined the *Wandervögel* in their attempt at a romantic escape from hated reality. His interest in literature was typical of what he sought: his favored readings were Ariosto's *Orlando Furioso,* Byron's poetry, and, already at an early age, Nietzsche's writings.

When Jünger was eighteen, he took the step from thought to action. He ran away from home to join the French Foreign Legion, with the intention of deserting after he had reached Africa. The Dark

Continent beckoned, calling him to the true, that is, adventurous life. (Accounts of former Legionnaires were avidly read by young Germans.) He had served for only about a month and had made one (abortive) attempt at desertion when his father secured his discharge by claiming his son's minority. Not only did he show solicitude, but also an unusual degree of paternal understanding: he promised Ernst a trip to Africa after graduation from high school. However, an event of global magnitude intervened: in August, 1914, World War I broke out. Although Africa receded from view and desire, it was never forgotten. Some twenty years later, Jünger gave a novelistic account of his adventure in *Afrikanische Spiele* (African Diversions [1936]). He had viewed Africa a year earlier, during a stopover while on a cruise; in the 1960's, he traveled in Egypt and the Sudan, in Angola and Morocco — more comfortably, and less adventurously, than he had anticipated decades earlier.

At the outbreak of the war, Jünger enlisted forthwith. He had taken the comprehensive examination requisite for high school certification; the requirements had been lowered owing to the "exigencies of the service." After two months of basic training, he was committed to the Western front, where he served for almost four years. When the war ended, he was a lieutenant in the infantry, a leader of its elite, the assault troops. He had been wounded seven times. In recognition of his exemplary valor, he was awarded the *Pour le mérite,* the highest military decoration. (Only fourteen infantry lieutenants were thus honored during the war.)

Jünger continued to serve for almost four more years — in the *Reichswehr,* the army of the Weimar Republic which, by stipulation of the Treaty of Versailles, was limited to a strength of 100,000 men. These years mark the beginning of his authorship, as he translated his war experience into the written word. The German High Command called on him to assist in the rewriting of training manuals, while his father prevailed on his son to expand the conscientiously kept diary into a novel.

In 1920, Jünger's first book appeared. Entitled *In Stahlgewittern* (In Storms of Steel), it renders an account of the war on the Western front after the rapid advance of the German army, almost to the gates of Paris, had been stopped. What the book describes are, therefore, the two phenomena that distinguish the first global conflagration from all other wars: (1) the *Stellungskrieg,* that is, trench or positional warfare; and (2) the *Materialschlacht,* that is, the battle in which the massive attack was to force the decision by the ever-increasing use of heavy weaponry, artillery in particular. It was this strategy which enveloped the battlefield in a "storm of steel." This prodigious massing of men and matériel did not resolve a stalemate of almost four years' duration. The war regained mobility only during its last stages, after the German effort had exhausted itself, with the American intervention tipping the scales.

Jünger's book sharply differs from the novels that have come to be thought of as representative of the First World War, books such as Henri Barbusse's *Le Feu* (Fire), John Dos Passos' *Three Soldiers,* or Erich Maria Remarque's *Im Westen nichts Neues* (All Quiet on the Western Front). They deal with the common soldier, whose life is the composite of boredom stemming from deadly routine, of discomfort entailing heat, cold, mud, vermin, and meager rations, of loss of identity or the feeling of being but a pawn in a senseless or, indeed, criminal game, of frustration and hopelessness aggravated by the ever-present threat of wound or death.

For Jünger, by contrast, war was a true quest for adventure. He was a soldier by inclination and temperament. Although it was but rarely fulfilled, his yearning was for the heroic exploit, for the encounter of man to man. When the rare moment came, he fully savored the excitement and the danger of the patrol in the exposed no man's land, in the assault of the shock troops he led, and during the great offensives when the war rose to a crescendo. He was there to confirm and reaffirm Heraclitus' dictum: war is the father of all things. At first he fought as the ardent patriot, doing his part to enhance the glory of his country. But when he came to realize that the war was lost and that the social and political order he had known lay in the throes of death, he convinced himself that this war was only the first link in a chain of global conflagrations, but that, in the end, a new and universal order would rise from death and destruction.

Jünger could not find a publisher for *In Stahlgewittern* because the early 1920's were years of revolution, of strong antiwar sentiment. Only after the book had been privately printed could the trade edition appear. It gained ever-increasing recognition; by the end of the decade its stature was firmly established. Jünger's first book also became his best known and most widely read publication, its numerous editions amounting to a quarter of a million copies. It has been translated into eight languages. No other book of Jünger's has attained such distinction.

In Stahlgewittern owed its growing recognition also to the several revisions to which the author subjected his first book, and which affected both its form and content. Increasingly, the facts were made to speak for themselves. The psychology of war, as Jünger understood it, was largely eliminated and made the concern of the essay *Der Krieg als inneres Erlebnis* (The Psychology of Combat [1922]). The excision of political pronouncements further enhanced the objectivity of the account, as did the deletion of polemical outbursts, notably those directed against pacifism and the bourgeois way of life. The author also refrained from criticizing the high command for adhering to outdated concepts of strategy and tactics, and he no longer upbraided the enemy when it had displayed a lack of valor.

The changes of the book's subtitle also bespeak increasing objectivity. Originally, it read "From the Diary of the Leader of Assault Troops." It was shortened to "A War Diary," thus eliminating the personal element. In the final edition (1961) the subtitle is omitted altogether. Although, in his collected works, the author still ranges *In Stahlgewittern* among his diaries, it deserves this designation only because it was based on, or grew from, regularly recorded events. Actually, it is an autobiographical novel since the protagonist is the author himself describing the interplay of the supraindividual event and an individual's fate.

I have stated that World War I was marked by "Stellungskrieg" and "Materialschlacht." *In Stahlgewittern* records one instance of positional warfare in the chapter "The British Attack." Since this event was particularly characteristic of the reality and the issues involved, Jünger wrote about it, expanding and elucidating in the process. The effort yielded a book of its own: *Das Wäldchen 125: Eine Chronik aus den Grabenkämpfen 1918.* (Copse 125: A Chronicle from the Trench Warfare of 1918 [1924]).

Copse 125 juts out from the German main line of defense. Thus exposed, it is subjected to increasing barrages and attacks and, conversely, defended with growing tenacity. The British finally take it by assault, but conquest and loss, victory and defeat, and the massive expenditure of men and matériel has been meaningless, as the stalemate is not broken.

One of the focal events described in the book is a patrol. Jünger, joined by one of his men, crawls through the wire entanglement into the bleak and battered no man's land. It is midday, and the danger of being discovered (and killed) is ever present. They finally sight a break in the trench connecting a British outpost with the main line of defense. The ambush seems interminable. At last, the soldier manning the outpost is relieved and, as he comes into view for an instant, is hit by the bullet from Jünger's rifle. The British open fire, but he and his comrade reach their line unscathed.

This patrol, unlike any other event, sheds true light on Jünger's career as a soldier. He had welcomed the war because he believed it would afford full play to his agonistic instincts, would offer him the opportunity to give account of himself in the man-to-man encounter. But in this war there was no room for chivalric combat. To prevail was not enough; the issue was killing. Massive destruction had replaced the victory of the individual. He would like to meet the enemy upright, in the open field; but instead he must crawl through no man's land and face nameless peril. He cannot come to blows with his adversary but must kill from ambush.

Yet Jünger's views were not shattered. Visiting an air base, he met the fighter pilots:

Battle is their great passion, the joy of challenging fate, of being fate. This they sense when, after the takeoff, they thrust themselves into uncertainty — a roaring flight of birds of prey. When they fly at heights from which the front lines are visible to them as no more than a thin network, and the fighters in the trenches as a mere string of points — then, in this venture of theirs, the fiery union of the spirit of ancient knighthood and the cold austerity of technology is consummated. It is granted to them to do battle with the world's best fighters in a new realm, in the sky hung with clouds. It is a deadly joust within whose lists there is only victory or the fatal plunge. Because of this, the battle is fought with the fury of raging beasts. (W, 1, 368)

The fighter pilots who combine soldierly virtue with technical skill are the knighthood of this war. This synthesis is basic to Jünger's evolving political ideas, which he fully developed in *Der Arbeiter* (1932).

The battle for Copse 125 is finally joined. The fighting is confused and seemingly without direction. In the darkness of the night, the *brouillard de la bataille* thickens. Friend and foe, barely recognizable, are both object and subject of a prodigious display of firepower:

Right before us a muffled cry is heard, then a snapping metallic click. An object, something like a piece of wood, falls on a mound and explodes almost immediately. And there is shouting, here and over there: many voices are sounded, confusedly, by masses of men. Flares, fired from Very pistols, rise up into the sir, a red glow which radiantly unfolds above us. A low sky filled with sparkling stars hovers over the scene of fighting. Hand grenades are defused, then thrown with no discernible target in sight. They detonate, forming one rolling thunder. Their impact shakes the trench, enveloping it in a snowy cloud of smoke. A yellow signal spirals upward, fiery scales breaking off, descending in ripples: it doubtless calls for a barrage. The British artillery responds at once, though the thunder is swallowed up in the general tumult. Before and behind us, the machine guns unloosen a storm of fire which envelops us in a mantle of cracking reports. . . . The rifle grenades whistle close by, past our steel helmets. Hand grenades, pushed within reach, are expended with incredible rapidity. Missiles in ever-increasing numbers fly circling into a cloud of silvery smoke, exploding in a shower of red stars. (W, 1, 442)

This is the way the "quiet" of trench warfare would erupt, enveloping a sector of the front in a raging storm of death-dealing matériel.

The companion volume to *Das Wäldchen 125* also appeared in 1925. It describes the author's role in that "Materialschlacht" of vast dimensions which opened the offensive of March, 1918. This account also expands a chapter of *In Stahlgewittern* ("Die grosse Schlacht"); its title is *Feuer und Blut: Ein kleiner Ausschnitt aus einer grossen Schlacht* (Fire and Blood: A Small Segment of a Great Battle).

The March offensive of 1918 was the last German attempt to force a breakthrough, to resolve the stalemate of three and a half years' duration. Initially successful, it ultimately failed. Jünger's military career culminated in those days. After prodigious preparations, the most massive artillery barrage ever, the battle was joined and masses of men were set in motion to meet the enemy on the shell-torn fields.

During the days preparatory to the battle, Jünger's thoughts turn to the state of the war. Though it has become a monstrously anonymous event, he reaffirms his conviction — in defiance of the forces that have reified the war — that the true soldier has remained an agent of his own, that an individual's decision and action are of ultimate account. The early enthusiasm has long been dissipated and the "courage of inexperience" has been replaced by the cool circumspection of the seasoned soldier. Though the battle may be lost and the hopes be shattered again, there is a faith that endures: this war, an event of such magnitude, has — must have — a positive meaning, although here and now it may not be clear what that is. Jünger believes in the ultimate "reason" of history. Looking forward

to the battle, he is stirred from contemplation and carried away by
the prospect of his taking part in

a fascinating game played at the ultimate bounds of life. We do not want a
peaceful and narrowly, rationally conceived world. What we do want in the
world, with everything it holds: its full measure of color and tone, its rich
melody, the tension of extremes. (FB, 1, 477)

Jünger serves history by indulging his propensities. He eagerly
yields to the lure of adventure, exuberant at the near prospect of all-
pervasive danger. "Life is the task, adventure its poetry. The sense of
duty renders this task bearable but the joy of facing danger lightens it
. . . we are not ashamed of being adventurers" (FB, 1, 478).

The spirit of exuberance is violently dispelled. On the march to the
assembly area in the darkness of the night, the guide loses his way.
An artillery shell hits the tightly grouped company, reducing its
strength by two-thirds, by one hundred men. Jünger, the commander, loses his nerve, running about aimlessly, finally regaining
his senses.

The battle begins the next morning. The barrage preceding the attack is more massive than ever. As it creeps forward, the attack is
mounted. The great battle splits up into limited engagements. The
advance is rapid, from time to time briefly interrupted by the
regrouping of forces, by moments of rest and orientation. But the
barrage, though it has reached the limit of its range, is not lifted and
thus stops the advance. (The almost impenetrable *brouillard de la
bataille* and insufficient means of communication made the high
command lose control of the action.) The following day, the battle is
resumed. Jünger is severely wounded and removed to a field hospital.

The book describing these events is justly called *Feuer und Blut,*
marking the elements of the great battles of World War I: prodigious
firepower supporting the attack of huge masses of men. The title also
suggests the fighting man's condition: his passion, blood's dark tur-
bulence, and his rational power attaining bright, fiery clarity are
fused to a wholeness of being.

In Stahlgewittern and the two shorter volumes, which elaborate on
the major phenomena of the war, record the external events while in
an essay, Jünger's first one, he sought to extract from them what they

meant. The essay is titled *Der Kampf als inneres Erlebnis* (The Psychology of Combat [1922]). It is an exercise in dynamic psychology, though its ultimate intent is metaphysical.

Jünger holds that the mainsprings of war are within us. The fearsome events that engulf the world from time to time reflect the warlike forces of the soul and manifest them in the event, in war. It is, in his opinion, inadequate to understand war as a social or political conflict which has become destructively acute.

Fathoming the human psyche, and penetrating to its depth, Jünger encounters *vis vitalis* (vital energy). This is the quintessential, metaphysical reality which is at once creative and destructive. Life is growth and decline, generation and destruction. However devastating the event (war, revolution, epidemic) may be, the regenerative force will always reassert itself. The splendor of rebirth equals the doom of death. Jünger always draws on the myth — as do the dynamic psychologists, notably Carl Jung and his followers — because the soul is understood as the repository of the living past, of man's myth-making impulse. After the Flood or the globe-consuming fire (Nordic myth), the world is recreated, its splendor renewed.

Jünger praises, indeed glorifies, war because here "life" reaches its highest pitch, that is, unleashes its energies freed from control and constraint. Furthermore, in battle, particularly in the encounter of man with man, the scales of being and not being are precariously balanced. How they will tip is a toss-up. During these moments, life reveals its essence and is thus fully and truly experienced. "Then I feel that being is ecstasy and life — fierce, mad, passionate — is a fervent prayer" (K, 5, 70). Jünger leaves no doubt that he holds the ecstasy of the fighting men to be a religious state: "In the fierce, merciless encounter, amidst fire and smoke, we [the adversaries] become one, body and embodiment of the same force" (K, 5, 101). Metaphysical insight has turned into a quasi-mystic reality. This conviction explains why Jünger never hated the enemy, never felt that destroying him was the sole or ultimate purpose. Though giving him no quarter, he loved him when he was bound to him in mortal combat.

The sense of oneness is general; so, too, are dream and reality indistinguishable.

In the nights of battle, I often felt that I was dreaming — dreaming of a legendary experience. I made my way through the trenches as though in dream, rationally unaware, oblivious to causal relations. And when the external reality, an event, obtruded the mind, I was hardly surprised. (K, 5, 95)

The present is felt to be a "legendary," or rather a mythic, that is, living, past. What is now has always been. The event (or the experience) may thus be recognized as archetypal. And yet another distinction is obliterated: "Illusion and the external world are one and the same, and he who offers up his life in error is still a hero" (K, 5, 105). The soldier may err in what he does and in his reasons for doing it, but fail he cannot because he is the "instrument of a higher reason." The historic event, war in particular, is always meaningful, because it ushers in a new phase of history. What this new phase, or era, is, becomes the object of Jünger's subsequent (and enduring) concern.

CHAPTER 2

Der Arbeiter

AFTER describing his soldierly exploits, Jünger set out to evaluate World War I as a political event and to see what the future was holding in store. This effort resulted in more than one hundred articles and essays which he published in right-wing journals, and some in book form too, in compilations to which kindred spirits also contributed. In both instances, he served as editor or coeditor as well. These activities culminated in the essay "Die totale Mobilmachung". (Total Mobilization [1930]) and a book entitled *Der Arbeiter: Herrschaft und Gestalt.* (The Worker: Rule and Gestalt [1932]).

The early articles are groping attempts at clarification. Jünger proceeds from the insight he had gained while the battles were still raging. For him, World War I was but the initial phase of a global conflagration. More wars, ever growing in scope and intensity, would inevitably follow. The events, properly understood, were metaphysical in nature: *vis vitalis,* the quintessential reality, manifested itself explosively and destructively at this juncture of history.

The analyses which Jünger made deal with three aspects of the postwar situation: the political issues at hand, the actions to be taken, and the relationship to be fostered with the *NSDAP*. Jünger held that the paramount issues were nationalism, socialism, militarism, and totalitarianism. However, he did not consider them as constituting a full and firm program to be realized by dint of uncompromising action. Issues were merely to serve the end of mobilizing the country's striking power. Nationalism is the ideology which ensures the people's cohesiveness — a requisite to success in war. Socialism removes social inequities, the major source of disunity and conflict, and, by means of total planning, will create the most powerful and efficacious war machine. Since war is the true issue, the military must be supreme, which means identifying the army with the state. No room for political differences can be allowed; decision-making must, therefore, be authoritarian (totalitarianism). It is Jünger's contention that the democratic processes are cumbersome as well as inefficient. What is to be achieved is simply the marshaling of the full measure of striking power.

Ideological radicalization is the prerequisite of proper action which, in the second half of the 1920's, called for unifying the radical right wing and winning additional supporters who, Jünger believed, could be recruited from war veterans like himself, workers who had not been alienated by Marxism, members of the youth movement, whose romantic idealism made them susceptible to a deeply irrational ideology, and all those who were hostile to the Weimar Republic. In this task of unifying and strengthening the right wing, the NSDAP was to play a major role. Although it gained support, and increasingly so as the worldwide depression of the late 1920's affected Germany disastrously, it did not, in Jünger's estimation, "mature" politically. Since he did not think it expedient to join the party, to work from within toward uncompromising radicalization (Hitler, at that time, steered a precarious course between legality and illegality), he proposed, quite unrealistically, a division of labor. The NSDAP was to organize the masses, whereas Jünger and his elite would function as "ideologues." Such a proposal was, of course, unacceptable to the Nazi leadership.

Jünger, on his part, was of two minds about Hitler. He recognized the efficacy of his oratory, accepted him as "der Trommler" (the drummer) who called the masses to the colors, but denied his claim to unquestioned, absolute leadership. Instead, he proposed, once again quite unrealistically, a "Zentralführerrat" (central council of leaders) to head the movement. This proposal was also rejected.

Jünger's political thinking culminated in a book which appeared just a few months prior to Hitler's advent to power. It was a notable success; fifteen-thousand copies were sold within a short time. Its somewhat perplexing title is *Der Arbeiter: Herrschaft und Gestalt.* Here, the word "Arbeiter," literally "the worker," has been endowed with a meaning quite its own. Although it designates the man who is destined to dominate and shape the future, its meaning differs from the Marxian conception. For this reason, the term will be used in the original German. "Gestalt" must not be understood psychologically, since Jünger conceives of the "Arbeiter" as an essentially metaphysical entity, or an archetype in the making. Moreover, the "Arbeiter" is therefore seen as a universal, not a specifically German, phenomenon. This will be shown further on. "Herrschaft," that is, "rule," is to indicate that the "Arbeiter" is destined to ascend to power on a global scale.

To begin with, and speaking generally: *Der Arbeiter* is a radical, unequivocal statement of militant totalitarianism. "Arbeiter" are all those who have understood that the world is undergoing a profoundly revolutionary change, who welcome that change, and who are willing to participate actively in this upheaval leading to global wars. Upon the conclusion of this universal civil war ("Weltbürgerkrieg"), the "Arbeiter" of the world will unite in establishing a global empire ("Weltimperium") to replace the nation states. It is characteristic of Jünger's "Arbeiter" that he is capable of performing the most demanding tasks, both destructive and constructive. However, Jünger wants the "Arbeiter" to be understood as being, ultimately, a metaphysical entity. Life, once again manifesting itself in cataclysmic conflagrations, has "created" the "Arbeiter," the fully cognizant, fearless soldier, as its agent. When the destructive impulse is exhausted, life will assert itself again creatively. Then the "Arbeiter" will turn the swords into ploughshares, to function as the engineer of global reconstruction.

Der Arbeiter, an essay of some three hundred pages, is divided into two parts. The extensive introduction, defining the basic concepts, is succeeded by the analysis of the present state of political affairs and a prognosis. In the first part, the author attempts to rid the reader of his middle-class preconceptions, holding that the bourgeois is incapable of penetrating to the quintessential reality, that is, life as metaphysically conceived. Ultimately, life is tantamount to the will to power. It is Jünger's conviction — a dubious one at that — that the middle class does not understand what power is and, therefore, never comes to grips with what he considers to be the paramount issue. The positive aspect of his course of instructions consists in making the reader *see* with the eyes of the "Arbeiter."

Since a metaphysical reality shapes the conditions that are and will be, the idea of personal (or individual) freedom is a delusion. Man is only free insofar as he rises above his condition, understands the inexorable course of events, and welcomes whatever will be. And so, paradoxically but logically, Jünger equates freedom with necessity. Man is either the conscious and willing agent or the blind, unwilling instrument of life's "will."

The idea that men are born equal and must be treated as equals before the law and in the conduct of political affairs is also rejected as a misconception. Yet equality there is — of those who serve that ineluctable power, and of those who are struck with metaphysical and, hence, political blindness. Since the issue is global war, requiring that the state be turned into an armed camp, equality is that of the uniform. Rank, on the other hand, is the measure of inequality. The autonomous individual answerable only to himself, is an illusory notion. This so-called individual is rapidly and inevitably replaced by what Jünger calls the "Typus": by men who are fashioned by serving the same supreme purpose.

Man is called upon to serve, fight, and immolate, thus shattering the bourgeois's love of security. Jünger insists that this pursuit bespeaks a failure to understand what "life" is and what it demands: willingness to face danger and readiness to make the ultimate sacrifice. The bourgeois try to escape the "will to power" and, of course, fail inevitably and miserably. By singling out the meek among them and making them representative of their class, Jünger simply chooses to disregard the power struggles — of all kinds — within civil society and the nation states.

Since there is no security, Jünger maintains, there can be no life of ease. Technology seems to provide the instruments of material comfort. It does indeed — until the machine is made to serve war. The quest for comfort must be abandoned, to be replaced by a willingness to serve and sacrifice. The search for peace is equally futile when war is always imminent, at least in this age of ours. Peace must be understood as a time during which preparations for war are made. This being fully understood, "total mobilization" will be the order of the day. Jünger's most advanced essay — it precedes *Der Arbeiter* by two years — develops this idea. It is entitled "Die totale Mobilmachung."

There is no ease, no comfort in an age governed by the idea and reality of work *(Arbeit)*, in an explosively dynamic age. "Everything must be understood as work: . . . the tempo of the brawn, brain and heart. Science is work, and so are love, art, worship, war, the dynamics of the atom and the force that moves the stars and the solar system" (DA, 6, 74). Everything is and must be work, to be intensified and accelerated toward one end, and one end only: preparation for global war ("total mobilization"):

From this realization stems a new human relationship: a more ardent love and a more awesome pitilessness. The possibility of a more serene anarchy, coinciding with the strictest kind of order, arises — a phenomenon already manifest in the great battles [of World War I]. . . . In this sense, the motor does not rule but symbolizes our time. It is the symbol of a force which combines explosiveness and precision. It is the bold toy of that type of man who blows himself up with abandon and who considers such an act as order confirmed. This attitude, of which neither idealist nor materialist is capable, is to be named heroic realism. It yields the full measure of aggressiveness which we need. Those who embody it are of the type of those volunteers who joyously welcomed the great war [World War I] and who have welcomed everything that succeeded, and is going to succeed, it. (DA, 6, 41)

"Everything": all the revolutions, both fascist and communist — not the attempts, because they are ultimately abortive, at broadening the democratic or the bourgeois way of life.

In the first part of *Der Arbeiter,* the author aims at disembarrassing the reader of his bourgeois views and preconceptions — not to engage him in arguments as to what is right and what is wrong, what is desirable and what is not, but "to cure him of his blindness": to make him *seem* capable of seeing the situation he faces.

What, then, is the situation? This is the concern of the second part of the book. Jünger claims to see (and this is one of his fundamental observations) that the so-called sovereign individual is dying. The war has wrought havoc on him, and the revolutions following it have aggravated the condition. The inflation (so disastrous in Germany) has destroyed the material basis. If the arts reveal anything, it is the dissolution of the worth and the dignity of the individual. In the final analysis, anonymous, that is, metaphysical ("seinsmässige") forces pose a momentous task: that of replacing the bourgeois with the "Typus des Arbeiters." *Hic Rhodus, hic salta.* Either adhere to outdated ideas and ideals and die a pathetic and ignominious death or be brave, identify with and promote the coming order of things. Those who most fully embody the "Gestalt des Arbeiters" constitute the governing elite; their vow is work, poverty, and bravery. These virtues are "far more profound" than the bourgeois ideal of self-realization ("Bildungsideal") (DA, 6, 200). This elite will form a closely knit, hierarchically constituted organization whose prototypes are the medieval Germanic orders of knighthood, the Society of Jesus, and the Prussian officers corps.

Jünger then poses the question as to how far technology, that is, the preparedness for war, has advanced. However, he is not so much concerned with weapon-making and military training as with the relationship of man and machine. It is essential that man identify himself with the technical tools, become as one with them. At this point, Jünger introduces the concept of "organische Konstruktion" (DA, 6, 197). The term connotes man's full, "natural" assimilation of the technical tool. Although he has progressed, and continues to do so, he has not yet reached the stage where the machine is to him as the limbs are to the plant and to the animal.

On the other hand, technology proves to be a radically destructive force. It destroys the traditional social groupings, such as the peasantry and the nobility. Jünger further holds that the machine is "the most resolute antichristian force yet to assert itself" (DA, 6, 171). Yet the "Arbeiter" is not without faith. It lies in the rediscovery that "life and worship ["Kultus"] are identical" *(ibid.)*. He venerates the primordial powers, i.e., vital energy in all its manifestations. The bourgeois is, once again, pointed to as a man without inner substance, at best an heir who squanders what has been bequeathed to him. His age is characterized by the progressive secularization of the human mind.

Jünger denigrates the bourgeois of his day. In the field of art, he is also "an heir and nothing but an heir" (DA, 6, 216). Artistically, he has lived in the past; that heritage is now dissipated. Since the so-called autonomous individual is dying, it follows that the artist, who epitomizes this idea, is also doomed. The modern schools and movements, the asseverations of their proponents notwithstanding, offer nothing but futile experiments or sterile innovations. The impetus is, therefore, quickly dissipated; hence the rapid succession of what are no more than fashions. In making these unequivocal assertions, Jünger clearly overreaches himself. He also tries to describe the obverse of the coin, what he calls "historical fetishism" (DA, 6, 217). It consists of an ever-accelerating "musealer Betrieb," an activity devoted to collecting and preserving true works of art.

As the age of bourgeois individualism ends, art ceases to be the supremely individual effort. Henceforth, it will not be a private but a public concern. Significantly, Jünger limits his anticipatory view to architecture. The eminent task confronting the "Arbeiter" will consist of refashioning the global surface with a view to obliterating the difference between city and country. It would not faze him if this undertaking were to lead to "dividing the earth's surface into hexagons (like honeycombs) or covering it with termite hills" (DA, 6, 252). Once again, he overstates his case when trying to show that the age of the "Arbeiter" utterly rejects the ideas and values of the past. But such is the stuff polemics are made of. In any event, the state, not the individual, will function as the "supreme architect" (DA, 6, 236). We

now know that Hitler and Stalin functioned as such — with disastrous results. Jünger might retort that their aesthetics was neither
radical nor original but jejune or epigonal.

Jünger wrote *Der Arbeiter* at what he believed to be a historic
moment: the imminent transition from liberal democracy to the state
of the "Arbeiter." In order to assure complete freedom of action, the
proponents of the new order were to cast off the shackles of the past.
Ideological issues were to be raised, but only as the means of mobilizing and revolutionizing the masses, to be used as weapons in the civil
war. Being captive of an ideology restricts freedom of action. There
must be no scruples. Whether an action is legal or illegal is immaterial, the only consideration being the promise or likelihood of
success. Control of political organizations and trade unions as well as
of the mass media must be obtained without regard to the means
employed. The leading echelon of the "Arbeiter" is free of doubt or
scruple. "Legal or illegal," "moral or immoral": these are middle-
class preoccupations. In such matters, Jünger and his adherents are
candid and honest, whereas — to their chagrin — the Nazi party
appeared to be running the risk of becoming captive of its ideology
and to be steering a precarious and confusing course between legality
and illegality.

Following the seizure of power, the social contracts ("Gesell-
schaftsverträge") will be replaced by the work plan ("Arbeitsplan").
The first term is misleading, and the second calls for amplification.
What is involved is, quite simply, the abolition of capitalism, the
"chaotic" free enterprise system (or what is left of it). It is to be
replaced by an authoritarian planned economy, planning being tantamount to "total mobilization." Complete preparedness is called
for because a global civil war ("Weltbürgerkrieg") is imminent. A maximum of independent striking power must be assured, a
minimum of vulnerability be striven for. Jünger, therefore, pleads for
an optimum of economic self-sufficiency, for a "fortress economy"
("Festungswirtschaft").

However, private property is not an ideological issue. The approach must be pragmatic. Such property will be retained "as far as
it can contribute to realizing total mobilization" (DA, 6, 302). At
any rate, it is imperative that the plan be flexible, readily adjustable
to changing conditions and, particularly, technological advances. In
assessing what science may yet provide for technology and, ultimately, the making of weapons, Jünger concluded (in 1930!): "Considering the state of nuclear physics, we note the distance still

separating technological practices from the optimum of its possibilities" (DA, 6, 192).

The totalitarian state replacing liberal democracy will introduce not only full military conscription but also "Arbeitsdienstpflicht," that is, the obligation of every man and woman to contribute to the state of general preparedness. To create an elitist cadre, special training centers will be established both in Germany and in occupied or conquered territories. In the course of the anticipated territorial expansion, whole populations will be resettled. And it is a matter of ready conjecture that "the ancient science of depopulation ["Entvölkerungspolitik," that is, genocide] will be rediscovered" (DA, 6, 158). The totally armed state will not have to engage solely in overt aggression but will be able to conduct "warfare without the use of powder" ("Krieg ohne Pulver") (DA, 6, 320). This is what *Revolverdiplomatie* is all about. Such measures and actions were soon to become reality. Jünger need not have doubted the radicalism of the Nazi party.

It was pointed out earlier that Jünger's political ideas stem from his war experience. They were confirmed by what he read, by Nietzsche and Spengler. Jünger read Nietzsche in his formative years; the influence was profound as well as enduring. He accepted the philosopher's radical criticism, the total rejection of what this age stood for: the capitalist system (paramount importance attaching to material gain and social prestige), the democratic form of government (promoting, in his view, the rule of mediocrity), positivism and materialism (a shallow way of viewing the world), and its art (lacking both substance and form). On the other hand, it was the quest for power and its corollary, the glorification of soldierly virtues, that confirmed Jünger's view gained in World War I. He may have found the seed of the concept of the "Arbeiter" in the *Will to Power:*

Concerning the future of the worker: Workers must learn to feel like soldiers. An honorarium, a salary but no wages. . . . The workers must learn to live as the middle class does now — but on a higher plane, that is, as the superior caste whose needs, however, are few. Hence they will be poor and live more simply. Power will be their sole possession. (Nos. 763, 764)

Spengler probably exerted a similarly strong influence on the fashioning of *Der Arbeiter*. Jünger read *The Decline of the West* upon publication (volume 1: 1918; volume 2: 1922), learning from it or at least being confirmed in his conviction that an age was drawing to its close and that the worldwide power struggle was to continue after the war. In a remarkable essay, entitled *Preussentum und Sozialismus* (Prussianism and Socialism [1920]), Spengler tried to "clarify" the burning issues of the day by defining (or redefining) certain basic concepts. He asserts (and this is fundamental to his thinking) that Prussianism and socialism are synonymous. It is his extraordinary claim that Friedrich Wilhelm I (1688 - 1740), the founder of the Prussian state, rather than Marx, was the first socialist. The ensemble of Prussian virtues — devotion to work, a sense of duty, willingness to serve the state — is, according to Spengler, what socialism is all about. The ultimate end which these virtues serve is power. Socialism *à la Prusse* aims at the enhancement of the power of the state, enabling it to assert itself beyond the frontiers. And it is the army that embodies this power. When Spengler says "Prussianism," he means state socialism, militarism, and imperialism. He asserts that "every German is a worker," while Jünger maintains that every German is in the process of becoming an "Arbeiter" and, rejecting his preceptor's bias, that the "Arbeiter" transcends all boundaries in that he is "Gestalt," archetypal.

In the midst of World War II, Jünger evaluated what he considered the first part of his literary career. "My books about the First World War, 'Total Mobilization,' *Der Arbeiter,* and also, at least in part, my essay on pain ["Über den Schmerz," 1934] — this is my Old Testament" (Str*, 166, deleted in subsequent editions). Although this comparison boggles the mind, it nonetheless shows what he thought of *Der Arbeiter*. He also indicated that "for years" he had been planning a "second" version, but that the book would have to stand as written. (Cf. Str*, 149. This statement was also deleted later on.) As a matter of fact, it is the only work of his that he has not revised. Instead, he wrote what may be considered the second part. *An der Zeitmauer* (By the Wall of Time) appeared in 1959, presumably a part of Jünger's New Testament. It will be discussed in due course.

A critique of *Der Arbeiter* must distinguish between what the book is and what its author takes it to be. It presents the case of militant totalitarianism, or of aggressive nihilism, clearly and honestly — very much in contrast to Hitler's *Mein Kampf* or Alfred Rosenberg's *Der Mythus des zwanzigsten Jahrhunderts* (The Myth of the Twentieth Century). Being a prognosis offered on the eve of the event, it bears out Jünger's claim that in writing *Der Arbeiter* he had performed in the manner of a "seismograph" (Str, 2, 13). But what he does not say in this connection is equally significant. The book also advocates and promotes the totalitarian upheaval. That it would have come to pass without his aid is true but unimportant.

Since polemics loom large in *Der Arbeiter,* they may tend to overshadow Jünger's true intent, which is philosophical. The result of his speculations is a metaphysics of history: a *Mythenschau,* that is, the envisagement of the myth in the making, of the "Arbeiter" as an archetype *in statu nascendi.* Jünger made this quite clear when he observed that, as "Gestalt," the "Arbeiter" is "a brother of Antaios, Atlas, and Prometheus rather than Hercules: a new Titan and son of the Great Serpent of which the demigod killed but a likeness" ("Maxima-Minima: Adnoten zum *Arbeiter"* [1964], 6, 357). It seems that Jünger here considers the serpent, the most ambiguous of symbols, as the embodiment of the earth. And similarly: "The 'Arbeiter' — like Antaios — is eminently of the earth, is its native son. His appearance is accompanied by upheavals which must be understood as tectonic. The night before his dawn is illuminated by the fire of the smithies. A divided earth is as loathsome to him as an artificial, confining garment" (*ibid.,* 345).

Jünger made these observations some thirty years after the publication of *Der Arbeiter.* Since there are numerous other instances where he reverts to, and elaborates on, the "Gestalt des Arbeiters," we cannot but conclude that it is the hub of his metahistorical speculations. The chapter "Toward a New Age" substantiates this conclusion.

CHAPTER 3

Afrikanische Spiele

*D*ER *Arbeiter* had not only anticipated but also welcomed the totalitarian solution. Now (1933) Hitler was in power.

New political regimes always try to muster the widest possible support. For obvious reasons, Jünger was urged to become a declared adherent. He was offered a seat in the *Reichstag* but declined. The *Dichterakademie* (the literary section of the Prussian Academy of the Arts) had been "cleansed" of its undesirable members, among them Heinrich and Thomas Mann. As it was being "gleichgeschaltet" (reconstituted along National Socialist lines), Jünger was elected to it: again he declined. When the *Völkischer Beobachter*, the party's most prestigious newspaper, reprinted some pieces of his *Abenteuerliche Herz* (Adventurous Heart), the author dispatched to the editors a blistering letter. He criticized them for not having obtained his permission and, more important, insisted, in general yet unmistakable terms, that their politics and his were different. (See Karl O. Paetel. *Ernst Jünger: Weg und Wirkung*, p. 241.)

The regime was not only irritated but became suspicious. The police searched his house. Since they found nothing that might have compromised him, Jünger made fun of them by "incriminating" himself. He displayed the *Pour le mérite*, the highest distinction for valor which he had been awarded in World War I.

What were the reasons for this surprising attitude? Prior to their coming to power, he had, though not without reservations, supported the National Socialists. But soon after the accomplished fact, he realized that a group of plebeians had taken charge; this hurt his aristocratic sensibilities. Their criminality soon became evident — to anyone who *wanted* to see. Clearly, the Nazi regime turned out to present a moral issue. And Jünger also foresaw that it would soon engage in a war that could only end disastrously. This was the kind of politics he feared and abhorred. It now was his kind of totalitarianism against that of the powers that be. In the afterword to *Afrikanische Spiele* (African Diversions, [1936]) — it was struck from later editions — he wrote:

There are indications that the elemental forces are about to come into play. The danger is becoming acute; there is little room for pedantry. We are entering upon a phase of history during which we will be living more naturally and, at the same time, more artificially — at any rate, more dangerously. . . . The order of things to come is not clear; our notions of it are indistinct, like the fading chords of distant music. We are well served by Théophile Gautier's fine dictum: "La barbarie nous vaut mieux que la platitude." This is, indeed, an alternative worth considering, particularly since one may well fear that people are favoring both at the same time.

Six years later, Jünger noted in his war diary *Strahlungen* how he understood Gautier's words: " 'barbarie' is best translated as 'nihilism' " (Str, 2, 444). The meaning appears to be that democratic humanism is a thing of the past and that those who try to uphold it utter platitudinous outcries. This is an age of nihilism; it behooves us to face up to this fact and find ways to overcome it. During the postwar years, Jünger tried to resolve this issue.

After 1933, he withdrew from politics. Since he thought the global conflagration imminent, he tried to put his house in order. However, nothing came of his plan to publish his collected works; the moment was not propitious. So he turned to more modest projects. In 1934, a collection of essays, some new and some old, appeared under the title *Blätter und Steine* (Leaves and Stones). One of these pieces, "Feuer und Bewegung" (Firepower and Mobility), deals with the paramount strategic problem of World War I when the rapid initial advance of the German army had been checked within weeks. Positional (or trench) warfare ensued. Both sides then attempted to bring about renewed mobility by employing ever-increasing firepower. These attempts failed, but attrition mounted, finally resulting in the collapse of the German forces.

Three of the essays relate to *Der Arbeiter*. In "Die Staubdämonen" (The Demons of Dust), Jünger incisively analyzes the work of Alfred Kubin, a truly creative genius. He concludes that this painter had made visible the decline and imminent dissolution of bourgeois society, as he had also done in his novel *Die andere Seite* (The Other Side [1908]). "Die totale Mobilmachung" has already been referred to. The third essay, "Über den Schmerz" (Concerning

Pain), deals with the "Arbeiter" as being exemplary owing to his capacity to endure pain. And in "Sizilischer Brief an den Mann im Mond" (Sicilian Letter to the Man in the Moon) he tries to recapture the moment during a voyage in Sicily (1929) which afforded him what he still thinks to be the decisive insight. This essay, being no less than the matrix of *Der Arbeiter*, is the most significant in the collection. Jünger, a stylist of note, is also a student of language. In "Lob der Vokale" (In Praise of the Vowels), he makes his first contribution to the study of symbolism in language. Inveterate traveler that he is, he also writes about his voyages. He is a keen observer of man and his ways; equally plastic are his descriptions of plant and animal. "Dalmatinischer Aufenthalt" (Sojourn in Dalmatia) is the first of numerous accounts of his travels, which will be dealt with in a separate chapter.

One hundred epigrams conclude the volume. Some of them are daringly critical of the regime. There is a difference, we read, between political histrionics and statesmanship. Those claiming to be statesmen are merely actors earning the kind of laurel that grows in hothouses. The Nazis claim racial superiority. Jünger informs them that "an inferior race exalts itself by comparing itself with other races, degrades them by comparison with itself." Concerning the use and abuse of power, he states: "A new technique in the use of violence may be considered as established after it has been tried out on the innovators."

An autobiographical novel on which Jünger had worked intermittently for three years appeared in 1936. It is entitled *Afrikanische Spiele*. The English translator renders "Spiele" as "diversions" which is correct, as the adolescent sought to escape the restrictions that family and school had imposed upon him, to live a life according to an image compounded of adventure and anarchic freedom. But with Jünger "Spiel" has a broader meaning. He has seen himself — throughout his life — as *homo ludens*, as a man for whom life is play, not to be devoted to working for tangible and respectable ends, such as social advancement, gain, prestige, security, and the like. Only if life is understood as an end in itself can it be lived truly and fully. No doubt, *homo ludens* is the very antithesis of the bourgeois, at least as Jünger saw him. The positivistic way of thinking is abhorrent to him because it denigrates the irrational. Utilitarianism bespeaks the shopkeeper's outlook. The pursuit of material gain is a waste of effort and energy. Social prestige is a hollow accomplishment.

By contrast, Africa loomed large, captivated him, attracted him irresistibly — but not all of Africa.

only the broad strip bisected by the Equator, true tropical country with its
awesome primeval forests and large rivers, its wild animals and peoples —
all that which is off the trodden path. I was happy in the thought that there
still was this kind of wilderness. (AH[1], 7, 43)

This is what he sought with mind and soul, a "land of happiness, of a
richer and more meaningful life, of passionate, bold dynamism, of
the great solitary adventure." Africa represented the "splendid anarchy of life" (AH[1], 7, 60; 45).

The boy had read everything he could lay his hands on about
Africa, including personal accounts of that organization which attracted misfits, outcasts, and rebels: the French Foreign Legion.

Discontent and disquiet mounted, the decision finally forcing itself
upon him. Toward the end of 1913, at the age of eighteen and less
than a year before high school graduation, he ran away. Making his
way to Verdun, he enlisted in the Foreign Legion, was taken to
Marseille and shipped to Algeria with a group of recruits. However,
he had no intention of exchanging the discipline of home and school
for that of the military. Once in Africa, he was going to desert at the
earliest possible moment, to seek the untrammeled life at the
Equator.

Afrikanische Spiele relates two attempts at desertion, both of
which were bound to fail. At the fort St. Thérèse (near Oran), he had
the opportunity to flee. He hesitated — and fell asleep. Upon waken-
ing, he mused:

I had faced, and been touched by, freedom, by solitariness, and it had been
too much. I was angry with myself, particularly over the fact that this mis-
erable fort had appeared to me as a warm nook, a place of greater security.
If this was the situation, then I would surely see the sun rise like this every
morning — for five years. I had suffered defeat, and at precisely the moment
when I had least expected it. (AS, 9, 116)

Later on, together with a few companions, he did desert. The
attempt failed. Betrayed by some natives, they were arrested by the
police and returned to the barracks. In the meantime, Jünger's father
had secured his son's release. The adventure had lasted less than two
months.

The boy had overestimated his strength. Romantic notions, the
quest for the exotic, could not carry him through — they were dispelled, inevitably so. He had just arrived at the training center in Sidi
Bel Abbès when he became acquainted with one of the time-honored
traditions of the military. If there is nothing for the recruit to do, a

job must and will be found. Idle Ernst was ordered to move a pile of rocks across the barracks yard. He was not rushed, and there it was:

a piece of Africa, the first one that I could contemplate undisturbed. I expected something special of this pile of rocks, though I couldn't say what it might be. Perhaps a golden serpent would suddenly emerge from it, slowly unwinding its coils. I waited patiently until the sun had almost set, but nothing, nothing of this sort happened. (AS, 9, 110)

Something similar happened to Jünger on the eve of his departure from Africa — appropriately concluding the romantic adventure. In the evening — it was already getting dark — he took a walk on the beach to collect shells (which was to become an enduring habit with him):

I was hardly surprised to see below me magnificently gleaming shells — a sight that only dreams vouchsafe: a whole bank of shells. The base was bluish, the shells glittering in bright colors. I eagerly rushed down. But when I got there, I was like one who had followed Rübezahl [the legendary man of the Silesian mountains who likes to fool the traveler]: The radiant treasure turned out to be a heap of live embers. (AS, 9, 180)

When Africa was, or was thought to be, casting its spell, nothing remained but broken stones and dying embers.

Jünger did not see much of the Dark Continent, but he saw and for a while lived with people such as he had not encountered before and would never meet again: rebels and outcasts, the "dregs of humanity," as the despicable bourgeois is wont to call them. There were those whose excessive vitality had driven them from society, as well as those who were inwardly broken, who had realized what they truly were or, rather, what they were not:

there is a kind of ultimate truth about every man, but he does not know it or does not conform to it, of which he must not be conscious. If, by some accident, this truth is revealed to him, it is as though the ground under his feet were caving in. He plunges into his own abyss, plunges down like a sleepwalker who is spoken to incautiously. (AS, 9, 76)

With Benoît, a comrade-at-arms, Jünger struck up a friendship which endured through the years. Benoît was one of the "natural sons of life" for whom civilization and its strictures are meaningless because they do not exist for them. For many years, he had lived, contentedly, in Annams' tropical forests; and he wanted to go back there. He was a Legionnaire but even the most rigid military discipline did not impinge on his inner freedom. Although without means, he lived the abundant life because his was the "spirit of money" (AS, 9, 100). Benoît knew the soldier's crude pleasures but preferred the joys of the mind which opium provides. Only some five years later, Jünger himself was to engage in systematic experimentation with drugs, the subject of the chapter "The Psychonaut." This was his first, though vicarious, experience. He listened enthralled to his friend:

It is difficult to describe this experience. It is as though, near the road, you catch sight of the entrance to a cavern. You enter, half curious, and half afraid, and there you see things as they appear to the eye on the bottom of the sea or in a strange or queer world. You hear unknown music; understand the meaning of words, encounter spirits that answer you. What is small appears enlarged, and what is large looks small. You can contemplate a flower for hours and see the world as an apple which your hand encloses. You walk through deserted cities full of palaces and monuments. You live in spheres where pain exalts you, where pleasure cuts up your heart. You learn to look down on the things of this world: fame, women, money, power. You are king in realms where you govern the course of the stars and the grains of dust. (AS, 9, 97)

Jünger revised the draft of *Afrikanische Spiele*, which was marked by "a positive solution." But even in the "final" version, the "romantic" element is not wholly suppressed. We read that the knapsack of Herbert Berger (the name which the author assumes in the novel) is stolen while he is absorbed in viewing the bay of Marseille (see AS, 9, 73). Benoît, whose real name was Rickert, remembers that the theft occurred while the recruit was busy sweeping the barracks yard. Later on, Dorothea, a dream figure and his guardian spirit, intrudes on his musings. She induces him to throw his revolver into the sea. However, Rickert recollects that "we sold the revolver and the stiletto in the city." The omissions are similarly significant. As noted earlier, Jünger, two of his companions, and Rickert were captured while trying to desert from the Legion. In prison, the latter proposed that they escape since he had succeeded in loosening the iron bars. However, they demurred; their "spirit of adventure was gone." (See Armin Mohler, *Die Schleife*, pp. 42 f.).

CHAPTER 4

Das abenteuerliche Herz

D   *AS abenteuerliche Herz: Figuren und Capriccios* (The
        Adventurous Heart: Figures and Capriccios), published
in 1938, is a collection of sixty-three short pieces of prose. Jünger had
drastically revised the original version, which, in the course of a
decade, had gone practically unnoticed. "I hear that it finds fifteen
readers every three months; such regularity is amazing," he wryly
commented (AH [2], 7, 180).

In the collected works, *Das abenteuerliche Herz* is ranged among
the "Essays," although this designation does not generally apply.
The original version is subtitled "Aufzeichnungen bei Tag und
Nacht," and justly so, because "notes" (or "informal record")
properly indicates that this rambling prose lacks clear form. "Bei
Tag und Nacht" suggests, on the one hand, that the phenomenon is
encountered consciously, in the light of day, and, on the other, that
the matter of concern is the nocturnal event. In the course of the revision, two distinct forms emerge, the "figure" and the "capriccio."
The "figures" are defined as "round pieces of granite which have
been smoothed in glacier mills, at high vantage points, where, in the
manner of engraved maps, the world appears a little smaller, though
also more distinct and regular, for the supreme order is hidden in the
multifaceted external world as in a *Vexierbild"* (AH [2], 7, 181). (A
"Vexierbild" is a puzzle in which an image is hidden in another.) The
writer is here concerned with individual objects or phenomena which,
by being acutely perceived and plastically described, reveal their
position in the order of things. By contrast, "capriccios" designate
acts, indeed, "excesses," of the unfettered mind, notably in dreams
(see AH [2], 7, 181,284). What Jünger has gathered together in this
volume, then, are adventures of the spirit, as the heart, the organ of
consummate cognition, understands them.

The venturesome spirit knows no restraints. He is at home in the open country as well as in the city. His quest encompasses the whole of organic and animate life: plant, animal, and man. He contemplates the object of his concern at the desk, in the garden, on walks, while traveling on land or sailing the seas. The essence of life is revealed to him by an insect as well as by an image of the divine. He contemplates the simple artifact and the astounding work of art. Colors are seen and symbolically understood. Man is observed in his everyday undertakings as well as in his sublime efforts. And there are the nocturnal encounters, visions and dreams, which are more productive perhaps than his diurnal endeavors.

What Jünger is about in what befalls him in his ventures is best shown by an interpretation of one of his accounts. I select the "figure" which opens the revised version of *Das abenteuerliche Herz:*

Die Tigerlilie
Lilium tigrinum. Sehr stark zurückgebogene Blütenblätter von einem geschminkten, wächsernen Rot, das zart, aber von hoher Leuchtkraft und mit zahlreichen ovalen, schwarzblauen Makeln gesprenkelt ist. Diese Makeln sind in einer Weise verteilt, die darauf schliessen lässt, dass die lebendige Kraft, die sie erzeugt, allmählich schwächer wird. So fehlen sie an der Spitze ganz, während sie in der Nähe des Kelchgrundes so kräftig hervorgetrieben sind, dass sie wie auf Stelzen auf hohen, fleischigen Auswüchsen stehen. Staubgefässe von der narkotischen Farbe eines dunkelrotbraunen Sammets, der zu Puder zermahlen ist.
Im Anblick erwächst die Vorstellung eines indischen Gauklerzeltes, in dessen Inneren eine leise, vorbereitende Musik erklingt. (AH [2], 7, 179)

The Tiger Lily
Lilium tigrinum. The petals arch back. The red color suggests rouge or wax; though delicate, it is highly radiant. From the pattern of the blackish blue speckles it may be inferred that *vis vitalis,* the vital energy which generates them, gradually decreases. The tips of the petals are lacking them, while below, near the bottom of the calyx, they are plastically distinct. As though on stilts, the speckles protrude from fleshy excrescences. The pollen is of a narcotic color, like reddish brown velvet ground to powder.
The sight conjures up the image of an Indic magician's tent; inside, soft preludial music resounds.

A flower is described, precisely and plastically, with cool scientific detachment. Briefly but significantly, the description gives way to metaphysical observation, as the phenomenon reveals its essence: *vis vitalis* is recognized as the generative force to which this plant owes its being. The concluding sentence brings about an abrupt change.

The image of the magician's tent suggests the symbolic significance attaching to the tiger lily. This is indicated some thirty pages later. On visiting a greenhouse exhibiting orchids in bloom, Jünger remarks: "It is, above all, the stanhopea which makes me linger — where, just as in the tiger lily, beauty and danger interpenetrate, though grandeur is lacking here" (AH [2], 7, 220).

What, then, precisely, is this symbol all about? That it is central to, and eminently characteristic of, Jünger's way of thinking is clearly indicated by the fact that "The Tiger Lily" opens this collection of "essays"; that it functions as a leitmotif.

A *flower* has been chosen to serve the symbolic purpose; and this is not fortuitous. Jünger has lived most of his life in the country, close to plant and animal — not just as an enchanted or sentimental beholder, but as a serious, metaphysically inclined student, a botanist, entomologist, and ichthyologist as well. While enrolled at the University of Leipzig, he combined the study of biology with philosophy.

Jünger's writings abound with references to plant life. Here are some representative passages:

The plants are among the world's truly silent, most mysterious entities. They sustain all life; they are the prototype of life. (AH [1], 7, 137)

I had long shown reverence for the kingdom of the plants, and during years of travel had tracked down its wonders. I knew intimately the sensation of the moment when the heart ceases to beat and we divine in a flower's unfolding the mysteries that each grain of seed conceals. (AM, 26)

While walking near Las Palmas in the Canary Islands (1936), he noted:

The very essence of plant life was revealed to me. These are perhaps the sublime moments in this world: receiving more than the embraces of beautiful women can give. I bent over one of these wonders of life. I struggled to catch my breath — a wave rising from the blue sea, breaking on me from above. A small flower is no less venerable than all the heavens. (Str, 2, 402)

And the dedicated gardener observes:

The whole of metaphysics rests in the kingdom of the plant. There is no better course in the invisible becoming visible than the annual cycle of the garden. (Str, 3, 256)

These passages, to which many similar ones could be added, are representative of Jünger's vitalistic metaphysics. War epitomizes the destructive power of *vis vitalis* whereas the plant in particular manifests and symbolizes its generative force and beauty.

Jünger follows a venerable tradition when he endows the flower with symbolic meaning. Owing to its short life cycle, the flower points up the brevity of life, as well as the transitoriness of beauty. But since the flower ever renews itself, cycle following upon cycle, it is also symbolic of duration. Thus, on festive occasions, the Greeks as well as the Romans wore crowns of flowers to exalt the joy and beauty of life, and they strewed flowers over the corpse, as it was carried to the pyre, and over the graves, thereby acknowledging that life is brief and fleeting. (By contrast, the Egyptians carried a skeleton to their banquets — to enhance the joy of life.) The flowers to which the widest and deepest significance attaches are the lotus (East) and the rose (West). It will be shown that in the tiger lily Jünger created a symbol that spans these two spheres.

The Indic lotus, *Nelumbo nucifera*, is a water lily. It is considered the mystic "Center" where Brahma dwells, as well as the visible manifestation of his occult activity. The lotus flower, growing out of the navel of Vishnu, the second of the divine trinity including Brahma and Shiva, symbolizes the universe, which grows from the central sun, that is, the central point or, in Aristotle's term, the "unmoved mover." The Creator is depicted as resting on the lotus, its structure being conceived as the symbol of the earth. In addition to its cosmic significance, the lotus specifically symbolizes eternal life, the sun, purity, and also the river Ganges. In Egypt, *Nymphea lotus* (also *coerulea*) stands for the Nile, for nascent life, or its first appearance. The lotus is viewed as a sacred plant not only in Egypt and India but also in China and Japan, and among the Aryans of Asia.

The rose, the preeminent floral symbol of the West, has, like the lotus, been associated with the mystic "Center," as well as with the heart, it being central to human life. This flower is also paramount in the garden of Eros, hence emblematic of Venus. In Dante's paradise, it assumes encompassing significance.

Dealing with the tiger lily, we observe, at the outset, that the name binds animal to flower. Though perhaps fortuitously, this fact expresses what Jünger calls "the inner and magic community of all life" (AH [1], 7, 173). The various entities of the external world are but emanations of the quintessential reality:

Look at the animal as though it were human and at man as a particular animal. Look at life as a dream among a thousand dreams, and at every dream as a particular insight into life. All this you can do if you hold the magic key. (AH [1], 7, 128)

Jünger's writings also abound with keen observations about animal life and with attempts at fathoming its mystery. On catching a species of the myriapods (millipedes) on the island of Rhodes (1938), he noted:

It will always be a deep joy to me to see for the first time and hold in my hands an animal that has been occupying my thoughts for many years. Such joy is coupled with the realization that here, once again, a particle of the stuff of life has assumed living form. All these forms, these marvelous creatures, we discover within us — unknown islands and magic reefs in our inner archipelago. Hence the happiness, and the shudder, that seizes us at their sight. (IF, 4, 220)

This belief was similarly stated in the original version of *Das abenteuerliche Herz*:

It is one of the moments of supreme wonder in our lives when life itself surprises us, when the animal appears on the scene . . . life embodied in mysterious figures — of solitary dancers performing to silent music. At such moments, man reflects deeply; he recognizes himself in the animal, identifying himself with it. (AH [1], 7, 123)

Such a magic view of plant, animal, and man, particularly the latter two, is rare in our time. Lest Jünger's view be judged as merely odd, it should be remembered that it revives beliefs that were commonly held for millennia and which, in his writings, have come into their own again. Prehistoric man engaged in sympathetic magic with the animals, particularly with those he hunted. By fashioning images (paintings, drawings, also, in rare instances, sculptures) of the animal, he believed he would gain power over it, thus assuring the successful hunt. Representations of wounded or killed animals were designed to propitiate their spirits. Some extant images were created to assure the animals' fertility. Totemism, too, is, or was, widespread; it is encountered in America, Africa, and the South Sea islands. "Totem" is a word meaning "my family mark" in the language of the Ojibwas, an Indian tribe in North America. An animal, and occasionally a plant or a natural phenomenon like fire, is believed to stand in a particular relationship to family or clan, subsequently also to an individual: the group or the individual has descended from the totem animal (or plant) and is named after it. It is held taboo. In time, the totem may assume human form, become visible as such.

Animal worship properly speaking springs from the zoomorphic conception of a deity. Its representations are threefold, often overlapping but clearly indicating the evolution of anthropomorphic conceptions: (1) the god assumes animal form; (2) it is represented as a human with an animal head; (3) it fully assumes human form, though vestigial animal features (horns, ears, etc.) remain — the animal itself is held sacred; (4) even though the deity is conceived as wholly anthropomorphic, it retains the ability to turn into an animal. Pertinent examples can be drawn from the religion of ancient Egypt, where, in the course of four millennia, a pantheon in which the animal assumed an exemplary and unequaled role arose. Sebec was the crocodile god represented as such a reptile or in human form bearing its head. Amon, the king of gods, is shown as a ram-headed man or as fully human, his head adorned with two plumes, the vestigial features of a bird. Among the Judges of the Dead was Amemait, the Devourer who punished the sinful. He is a composite of three fearsome animals, the lion, the hippopotamus, and the crocodile.

The belief in the cosmogonic power of the animal is universal. Thoth, or the ibis, created the world. Among the Algonquins, the Great Hare is the supreme creator. The Babylonians believed that the Serpent Kishar fashioned the earth while Anshar, its counterpart, brought forth the sky.

These cosmogonic speculations help explain why a good many stellar constellations are named after animals. The Zodiac is the prime example. Although it is commonly named the Wheel of Life, the word actually means "circle of animals." However, only seven of the twelve stars are named after animals. Most of these, such as the ram (Aries), the bull (Taurus), the lion (Leo), scorpion (Scorpio), or fishes (Pisces), bear symbolic significances transcending the astrological mystery.

Turning to the hero who holds a position between man and god, we find that the myth surrounding him involves very frequently encounters with animals. So Hercules, who confronted the animal in nine instances of his "Twelve Labors." Siegfried, the Nordic hero, was physically inviolate after immersing himself in the blood of the dragon he had killed. And there is the Christian hero: Michael and George, both valorous saints, are depicted as slaying this monstrous beast. By contrast — and this points up a significant characteristic of the symbol, that is, its ambiguity — the dragon plays an entirely different — indeed a supremely creative — role in Eastern thought. In China, it represented both earth and water, above all the fertilizing power of rain.

It may, of course, be argued that the dragon is a fabulous beast and therefore not of the animal world. However, since it is a creature of the imagination, it is thought to be the animal *par excellence.* For this reason it is not restricted to any particular or unequivocal form: the oldest Chinese images of the dragon clearly resemble the horse, whereas in the medieval West it is depicted as composite of eagle, serpent, and bat. And since it is the animal epitomized, it can be evil or beneficent. It may even be made to obey after being overcome, as in the case of St. George's struggle with such a monster.

Saints battling the fabulous beast, St. George among them, lead us to observe that the animal does not preoccupy exclusively pagan thinking, though it is true that Christianity reduces (or elevates — depending on one's point of view) it to the level of symbol or allegory. An early Christian symbol is the fish. The Greek word for it is *ichthys;* its letters, fully spelled out, yield: Jesus Christ, Son of God, Saviour. Allegory is served by the pelican which, according to ancient belief, so greatly loves its young that it feeds them with the blood flowing from the self-inflicted wound of its breast. This sacrificial love was likened to that of Christ, who is shown also as an animal, as the lamb that God sacrificed to save man ("Agnus Dei"). This, incidentally, shows how Christian thought assimilated the ancient and universal practice of animal sacrifice.

In literature, the "magic community of all life," of which Jünger speaks, is clearly and fully exemplified in the folk tale (Märchen). It is also truly representative because such tales are universally told. For the problem at hand, the relationship of man and animal, the collection compiled by the Grimm brothers, *Kinder- und Hausmärchen,* may serve as typical and characteristic.

To begin with: the vast majority of these two hundred tales involve animals. Man and animal live a life together, virtually on the same plane, as equals. The community is close because the partners freely communicate with each other. The animals speak as the humans do or, at least, understand their idiom. There is no barrier either where the animals speak their own language: the willing and patient human does readily understand them. The protagonist in "The Three

Languages," a guileless fool, learns to understand what dogs, birds, and frogs say.

Metamorphoses are common: man changing to animal, and back again to man. In "The Frog King," the prince is changed to such an amphibian; the princess, in turn, lifts the spell. The animal may be wicked, like the wolf in "Little Red Riding Hood," or beneficent, like the doves which help Cinderella perform the impossible labors demanded of her and also provide her with glamorous attire. "The Valiant Little Tailor" attains the stature of the mythic hero by outwitting giants and prevailing over a wild boar and the unicorn.

The preceding observations are intended to serve a dual purpose: to amplify what is meant by "the magic community of all life" and to show how the consideration of any meaningful symbol leads to the formation of an associative chain. Such concatenations prove the symbol to be fruitful; therein lies its ultimate significance.

Now turning to the tiger lily, we consider the constituent elements of this name. In the East, the lily to which symbolic meaning has accrued is *Lilium candidum,* the white lily. It was sacred to Juno and also an attribute of elves and fairies. To the Jews and, subsequently, to the Christians it was symbolic of purity. The Holy Virgin and some of the saints are depicted holding a lily. Graves are adorned with it to symbolize the hope of eternal life. In stylized form, it gained heraldic significance as the fleur-de-lis.

This flower loses nothing of its beauty when its coloration changes from white to red and black; but then its gentleness is transformed into fierceness and, according to Jünger, the danger which it entails. Although in the West the tiger is associated with Dionysos, being also symbolic of wrath and cruelty, it is the Far East that, by contrast, accorded creative and truly cosmic significance to this animal. In China, the Five Tigers are the defenders of the global order against the forces of chaos. Four of them are identified with the four seasons, the cycle of life, and its renewal. In spatial terms, their spheres of dominance are the four quarters of the globe. The fifth Tiger inhabits the earth, reigning supreme over the others. Its *locus* is the "Center," as the Emperor is situated at the center of the world. However, the tiger also symbolizes darkness, that is, the base powers of the instinct, the beast in man. What, rationally speaking, is ambiguous or mutually exclusive, is actually an image showing the ultimate oneness of opposing cosmic forces.

Red is the dominant color of the tiger lily. Jünger describes it with precision — its particular tone, value, and texture. Being also aware of the symbolism of color, he included in *Das abenteuerliche Herz* an essay on the color red, which, in the most general sense, is the color of life. Thus blood, the life-sustaining fluid, is red. Almost inevitably, it signifies love and sex in both their exalted and degraded forms. Red is the color of fire, a creative as well as a destructive element. Blood is shed on the battlefield and offered up at the sacrificial altar. (The wine of the Eucharist is, or at least signifies, the blood of Christ.) Red is the color of the deity and the devil, of divine love and sin, of legitimate power and rebellion.

The black speckles of the tiger lily indicate a decrease of the vital energy. This color is, indeed, symbolic of dissolution, putrefaction, and, ultimately, death, but also of the earth and of fertilized land. Jünger considers the black rose the mystic symbol of being, of the oneness of life and death.

"The sight [of the tiger lily] conjures up the image of an Indic magician's tent; within soft preludial music resounds." An object has been contemplated and described, and now, suddenly, abruptly, an image obtrudes itself on the writer's mind. Commenting on sudden changes of this kind, Jünger writes: "This moment, when one phenomenon superimposes itself on another, when what is unexpected, thoroughly different, emerges, marks our entry into the demonic world" (AH [1], 7, 205). The contemplation of an object is being transcended, leading into the realm of the demons, of good and evil spirits. The two worlds, the natural and the supernatural, are not wholly separate. Not only are they contiguous; the line that divides them is imaginary and may, therefore, be readily transversed. What we actually face is not two worlds but two spheres of one and the same world. Changing from the observation of an object to the realization of an image involves no more than moving from one sphere to another, the "magic change" as Jünger calls it. Actually, no change, no metamorphosis (flower to tent) occurs. The "magician" is precisely that man who is simultaneously at home and at work in these two spheres. He is endowed with "two pairs of eyes": the one to perceive the external world, that of bodies, and the other to visualize the realm of the spirits: "The real is as magical as the magical is real."

Finally, the title of the book, *Das abenteuerliche Herz,* needs to be pondered.

Only when the *heart* [E.J.'s emphasis] takes command of the army of our thoughts, only then do facts and statements reveal their worth and significance. Only then do they fully echo life's hot breath. (AH [2], 7, 97)

In traditional ways of thought, the heart was taken to be the true seat of intelligence, the brain being merely instrumental. Or, metaphorically speaking, the heart is to the sun as the brain, its satellite, is to the moon. Since the heart is the epicenter of the mind, its grasp is undivided; it is also complete. Only the heart truly comprehends (*com* — together; *prehendere* — to seize). By contrast, both intellect and reason accomplish comprehensiveness only by dint of successive acts, a concatenation of efforts. Surely, the heart comprehends, cannot but comprehend, individual phenomena or entities, but it does so always within the context of the whole.

Yet, Jünger's trust in the powers of the heart is coupled with an awareness of its insufficiency: man is capable of knowing, but ultimate knowledge is denied him. Though clearly in view, the goal can only be approached, but never reached. But the true metaphysician may summon help, the "help of the demons" (AH [1], 7, 155), of spirits good *and* evil, because he is a magician, master of the mysterious but also hazardous venture. This observation sheds light on the import and meaning of the image that concludes the essay, on the image of the magician's tent.

We conclude: the two symbols, the adventurous heart and the tiger lily, elucidate each other. The heart is the seat of *vis vitalis,* manifesting itself visibly in the red flower. Red is also the fluidum of life which the heart renews. But the heart is the organ of comprehensive knowledge as well, the tiger lily putting its power to the test. So the heart embodies the whole of life in a single flower. In the process, the tiger lily is raised to the stature of a symbol, for even the most familiar, everyday phenomenon may be understood as quintessentially significant (see AH [1], 7, 96).

The symbol results from interaction, of the senses and the feelings, of intellect and reason. It is a process in which the heart "takes command." The tiger lily is a significant symbol — at least as far as Jünger's world is concerned — because it embodies life in its variety and contradictoriness *and* its ultimate unity. It encompasses — or, at least, suggests — the realms of plant and animal, male and female, love and vice, legitimate power and rebellion, life and death, "beauty and danger."

A true symbol is rich in meaning; hence its ambiguity. It is basic to its understanding that, underlying these ambiguities, we recognize the relationship of what is transitory to what is enduring. What is eternal reveals itself in the temporal, and what is invisible is manifest in the visible. Every phenomenon partakes of two such qualities (Cf. SK, 8, 57).

Jünger is among those modern writers who re-create their views by dint of the symbol. Since tradition no longer sustains them, the ancient images having lost their meaning or cohesion, they must strike out on their own. The difficulty they encounter is not so much the demand of creativeness but rather the absence or lack of a generally binding view of the world. It is to be borne in mind that the symbol is an eminently sociological phenomenon. Through it, a group expresses what binds it together and what motivates it; in it, their members recognize each other, and, through it, they speak to each other. Thus the poet of the Middle Ages centered his ideas and beliefs and those of the group of and for which he spoke (knighthood) on the Holy Grail — just as the cross and, earlier, the fish, served as the binding symbol of Christendom. By contrast, the poet of our days stands alone, "an Island intire of it selfe" (Donne), does not know to and for whom he speaks, is beset by doubts, if indeed he is wanted to be heard. This lack of inner, spiritual cohesiveness, a characteristic of modern society, helps explain the paucity, or even the absence, of "unifying" symbols. Yet, despite the adverse condition, the poet of our time attempts to express himself in and through symbols because he speaks not only for himself but for others — or so he thinks or must think. Yet his symbol cannot be more (or only little more) than the image of one (isolated) individual's world. Thus comes about the "subjective symbol" or cypher — the paradox of our age. It is, for a number of reasons, hard to understand. Since it is the expression of an highly individual idea, stance, or condition, it is difficult for the reader, being truly an outsider, to relate to it, to identify himself with it. Furthermore, the poet, partaking of the cultural heritage, draws also on the symbolism of the past. And this he often does in a sovereignly creative if sometimes arbitrary fashion. In the process, new meaning accrues to an old symbol. But this new meaning must be made clear, or at least suggested, and this he can only do unobtrusively — by playing the key of understanding into the reader's hands. The poet can thus expect to be understood without "unpoetically" explaining or elaborating.

CHAPTER 5

Auf den Marmorklippen

A few days prior to the outbreak of World War II and before being called up to serve again, Jünger finished a short novel which proved to be an almost shocking sensation and has remained a challenge to critics owing to its baffling complexity. *Auf den Marmorklippen* (On the Marble Cliffs [1939]) cries out political protest, expounds a philosophy of history, is an exercise in autobiography, knits a web of symbols, and exemplifies "surrealism."

As is typical of Jünger's fiction, the setting of this novel is of the author's making, although his imagination was enlivened by memories of what he had seen in Southern Germany, on the Dalmation coast, in Athens and along the Isthmus of Corinth, on Corfu and Rhodes, and in Rio de Janeiro:

It is incumbent on a writer to travel a good deal — to find out what the earth has to offer. Then the impressions must blend and begin to flow like honey gathered from different flowers. The mind derives its nourishment only from the elements of memories. (Str, 2, 34)

The center of this composite, yet wholly integrated, scene is formed by some spurs of rock, the marble cliffs. They afford a full view of the land about: the Marina, a coastal region, and the seat of an urban civilization. Beyond the waters lies Alta Plana, a mountainous plateau. Flatlands unroll in the opposite direction, the Campagna of the farmer and the herdsman. This side of the horizon, the view gathers in virginal land: swamp and primeval forest. It was the author's intent to create a scene composed of basic topographical features, for city and country are conceived as the constituent *loci* of human habitation and activity. Not elaborated individuality but sparse, almost mythic typicality is the hallmark of the scene, thus according with the plot and the ideas of the narrative. Their contemporaneity is not to be denied, but their significance is to be understood as typical and ever recurring.

The time of the fictional event is also ambiguous. The sense of the past, of an age antedating the machine, is strong; but there is talk about the airplane, and an automobile makes its way to the foot of the marble cliffs. Christianity is made to coexist with paganism as a viable force.

An anonymous narrator and his brother Otho are the protagonists. They have resigned from military service and withdrawn from political activity in the "Mauretania," an organization pursuing totalitarian aims. They now live in seclusion, in the hermitage atop the marble cliffs, devoting their time to botanical and linguistic studies and the pursuit of quintessential truth. However, this life of contemplation is threatened and finally terminated by the developments below: the subversion and, ultimately, destruction of the social order.

One of the proponents of subversion is the Chief Ranger, a powerful, even charismatic personality who has gained ascendency also by instilling fear in the people, through intimidation and overt terror. His aim is the destruction of civilization and the reduction of social order to primitivistic anarchy upon which he will then impose his absolute rule.

Braquemart is the Chief Ranger's rival. Although both are bent on destroying the existing order, they differ in their views as to how to replace it. This rival is an intellectual, a disciple of Nietzsche's — Jünger refers to the philosopher as the old "Pulverkopf," an explosive mind — who propounds an icily cerebral nihilism, whereas the Chief Ranger embodies the chthonic forces, intending "to people the Marina with wild beasts, while Braquemart looked on it as land to be settled with slaves and their overlords. . . . Between full-blown nihilism and unbridled anarchy there is a profound difference. Whether the abodes of man shall become desert or primeval forest depends upon the outcome of this struggle" (AM, 82). (Reality, which is threatened by demonic forces, is safeguarded by the life cycle of the plants. Gardeners and botanists are therefore the Chief Ranger's true opponents.)

Braquemart and the Chief Ranger are but ineffectively opposed by the legally constituted powers, because the body politic is weakened after a lost war and has been paralyzed by growing subversion. However, there are focal points of opposition. Prince Sunmyra represents the forces of conservatism. Considering the Chief Ranger the more dangerous of the revolutionaries, he has entered into a tactical alliance with Braquemart. The Prince is the exponent of the power of the spirit, while Belovar, another ally, jealously safeguards the freedom of farmer and herdsman. Instead of rising to the issue, the intellectuals and, in particular, the poets have violated their trust by siding with the antihumanistic conspiracy. The armed forces feign neutrality; they will be "loyal" to the victorious faction.

The Chief Ranger strikes first — to end the rivalry between "anarchy" and "nihilism." Braquemart (and Sunmyra) fall victim to his terror. Captured, they are taken to a camp of torture and execution called "Köppels-Bleek," that is, "where the heads bleach" (see Str, 3, 451). There they are decapitated, their heads planted upon spiked poles.

This is the signal for the two brothers to join Belovar's forces in their fight with the Chief Ranger. The battle is fought at night, flaming torches providing sparse and erratic illumination. The main contingents are packs of dogs — Belovar's bloodhounds, bravely but futilely engaging the Chief Ranger's mastiffs. The nocturnal engagement is fought with bestial cruelty, which is typical of any civil war. This is the quintessential meaning of the horrendous encounter: "Thus in human history there ever occur moments in which it threatens to come under the sway of none but demonic forces" (AM, 97). Thus the author avoids a narrowly religious interpretation of the event. Again the Chief Ranger prevails.

The two brothers make their way back to the hermitage atop the marble cliffs — relentlessly pursued by the battle-crazed mastiffs. And now a second encounter of beast with beast occurs, that between the dogs and the lance-headed vipers, the embodied guardian spirits of the brothers' abode. Strength and ferocity are no match for the lightning thrust of venomous strength. Jünger later commented: "In this battle of the dogs with the serpents I envisioned the encounter of blood and one of its quintessences, that is poison" (Str, 2, 53).

At the same time, the Chief Ranger's hordes lay waste to the land. The nameless brother views the conflagration:

Nun war die Tiefe des Verderbens in hohen Flammen offenbar geworden, und weithin leuchteten die alten und schönen Städte am Rande der Marina im Untergange auf. Sie funkelten im Feuer gleich einer Kette von Rubinen, und kräuselnd wuchs aus den dunklen Tiefen der Gewässer ihr Spiegelbild empor. Es brannten auch die Dörfer und die Weiler im weiten Lande, und

aus den stolzen Schlössern und den Klöstern im Tale schlug hoch die
Feuersbrunst empor. Die Flammen ragten wie goldene Palmen rauchlos in
die unbewegte Luft, indes aus ihren Kronen ein Feuerregen fiel. Hoch über
diesem Funkenwirbel schwebten rot angestrahlte Taubenschwärme und
Reiher, die aus dem Schilfe aufgestiegen waren, in der Nacht. Sie kreisten
bis ihr Gefieder sich in Flammen hüllte, dann sanken sie wie brennende Lam-
pione in die Feuersbrunst hinab.

Als ob der Raum ganz luftleer wäre, drang nicht ein Laut herauf; das
Schauspiel dehnte sich in fürchterlicher Stille aus. Ich hörte dort unten nicht
die Kinder weinen und die Mütter klagen, auch nicht das Kampfgeschrei der
Sippenbünde und das Brüllen des Viehes, das in den Ställen stand. Von allen
Schrecken der Vernichtung stieg zu den Marmorklippen einzig der goldene
Schimmer empor. So flammen ferne Welten zur Lust der Augen in der
Schönheit des Unterganges auf. (Werke, 9, 287)

Now the extent of the destruction could be read in towering flames, and far
and wide the old and lovely towns along the Marina stood bright in ruin.
They sparkled in fire like a chain of rubies, and from the dark depths of the
water there rose their shimmering image. The villages and farms, too,
burned throughout the land, and from the proud castles and cloisters in the
valley the fires shot up. The flames towered smokelessly like golden palms
into the unstirred air, and from their crowns there fell a golden rain of fire.
High above this whirl of sparks, touched with red light, flocks of doves and
herons which had risen from the reeds soared in the night. They circled until
their plumage was enveloped in flames; then they sank like flares into the
blaze.

Not a sound rose up to me, as if all space were devoid of air; the spectacle
unfolded in terrible silence. Below me I could hear neither the children weep-
ing nor the mothers wailing, nor the war-cry of the clans nor the bellowing of
the cattle in their byres. Of all the terrors of destruction, only the shimmering golden light of the flames rose up to the Marble Cliffs. So distant worlds
flared up to delight our eyes in the beauty of their ruin. (AM, 106)

This descriptive passage reveals the author's ultimate intent. Not the
immediacy of the political event, or the wider, representative
significance of the historic occurrence, but the myth as palpable, inexorable reality is what *Auf den Marmorklippen* is ultimately about:
the world will periodically be destroyed by fire, to be resurrected
afresh. This is the meaning of the Heraclitean fire, as well as of the
global conflagration of the Germanic myth ("Weltenbrand").

The passage just quoted merits analysis because it is stylistically
typical of the story at hand. The protagonist who observes the event
is described as detached from its horrors, but not wholly so. He
seems to indulge his aesthetic propensities, seems taken by the

beauty, indeed the splendor, of the pyrogenous destruction. He observes from a distance that the burning cities "sparkled in fire like a chain of rubies." But the sentence continues: "and from the dark depth of the waters there rose their shimmering image." Obviously, the rippled surface of the water cannot be discerned from the observer's distant vantage point. The fires also engulf the animals. Doves and herons circle above the burning buildings until they drop, their plumage "enveloped in flames." The ornithologist knows nothing of such self-destructive behavior. However, inconsistencies of this kind are readily resolved if the final event of the novel, the destruction of a whole civilization, is described as seen — or at least conceived — in a dream. Here space is perceived as by the wakeful eye and, at the same time, as compressed or telescoped. The unusual behavior of the birds fits the dream, but it may also be understood as symbolic of the untoward event.

Through his use of language, Jünger creates a sense of tension. In the first paragraph, the polarity is between movement and rest. The fires "shoot up," the image of the burning cities "rises," and the birds "soar" into the night. The upward movements are balanced by instances of falling: golden rain of fire "falls," and the burning birds "sink" like flares. And moments of immobility contrast with movement. The Marina "stood" bright in ruin, and the flames "towered" above the scene.

The tension in the second paragraph does not stem from a concatenation of perceptions, but from the observer's reflections or reactions. He is enveloped in an awesome silence but cannot help but sense the "crying" of the children, the "wailing" of their mothers, the "war-cry" of the embattled fighters, and the "bellowing" of the crazed cattle locked in burning barns.

A third type of tension is created by the dialectic of destruction and beauty, of involvement and detachment. "So distant worlds flared up to delight our eyes in the beauty of their ruin." A word of Léon Bloy's, noted by Jünger in his diary of World War II, provides the fitting commentary: "Dans l'état de chute, la beauté est un monstre" (Str, 3, 596).

Auf den Marmorklippen is clearly an act of resistance and an accusation, a thinly veiled criticism of totalitarian nihilism. It describes the factional strife within this movement which, in Germany, reached its climax in 1934 when Hitler crushed an opposing faction with ruthless violence. The author shows up the terroristic practices by graphically describing a camp of torture and murder. However, the parallel is not precisely historical because the camp is shown to exist already prior to the Chief Ranger's seizure of power. The base opportunism of a substantial segment of the intelligentsia is pilloried: its betrayal of the humanistic tradition, its denigration of the arts and their subversion to mean political ends. We need only note that a good many poets and professors sold out to the Hitler regime; *le trahison des clercs* was not confined to isolated instances. Jünger, the highly decorated soldier of World War I, castigates the military for its cowardly "neutrality" during the struggle for power and its opportunistic declaration of "loyalty" after the fact. This is, in essence, the history of the *Reichswehr* before and after 1933.

Conversely, Father Lampros, that is, "the radiant one," is made splendidly to represent Christian religion and the institution of the church — both objects of attack by the National Socialists. The priest is crushed by the collapse of the burning monastery; Prince Sunmyra, the proponent of conservatism, is murdered outright. It should be remembered that Hitler not only liquidated the opposing faction within his own party but attacked with equal ferocity the forces of the spirit and of tradition. Jünger does not fail to reaffirm, and unequivocally so, the tenets of the humanistic tradition: "There is a trinity of word, liberty, and the spirit" (AM, 63). And again: what is "at stake" is "life in its highest form, liberty, and the dignity of man" (AM, 84).

How was it possible that such a book could be published in Germany in 1938? Perhaps it was not subjected to censorship because Jünger was known as the author of *In Stahlgewittern, Die totale Mobilmachung* and *Der Arbeiter* and was, therefore, not suspect. But this hardly holds because Jünger had made it clear in his communications to the *Völkischer Beobachter* and the *Deutsche Akademie der Dichtung* (see p. 40) that he did not want to be counted among the supporters of the Nazi regime. And so one may surmise that the censors were inept — as they often are — having failed to penetrate the thin veil of allegory. When the damage was done, it was probably thought prudent not to enhance the book's appeal by condemning or suppressing it outright. In the course of the war, the book was in increasingly short supply: less and less paper was allotted for new printings, and finally, none at all. Since Jünger, now again wearing the uniform, enjoyed the protection of certain high-ranking officers who opposed the Nazi regime, an edition for the armed forces *(Wehrmachtsausgabe)* of twenty thousand copies was issued as late as 1943.

Auf den Marmorklippen is thus to be counted among the significant literary contributions of the so-called *Innere Emigration* — of those writers who opposed the Hitler regime but chose to remain in Germany. This group includes, among others, Werner Bergengruen, Reinhold Schneider, Günther Weisenborn, and Ernst Wiechert.

Though the novel appears to be remote in time and place, and its characters may strike the reader as wholly fictional, it nonetheless bears clearly autobiographical traits. Thus the nameless narrator is reminiscent of the author himself. He, too, had served in the war and was active, like Braquemart and the Chief Ranger, in a radically rightist organization. Like Jünger, he had withdrawn from such activities to devote himself to botanical studies, the symbolism of language, and metaphysical inquiries. Otho, the narrator's brother, shares this past and these present interests. His prototype is the author's brother, Friedrich Georg Jünger, who is also a noted author, of fiction, poetry, and essays. Biedenhorn, the commander of the army, is fashioned after one of the author's brothers-in-law. The prototype of Prince Sunmyra is Count von Trott zu Solz, who, some years after Jünger had met him, was implicated in the abortive attempt on Hitler's life (July 20, 1944); he was summarily convicted and executed.

Unquestionably, Jünger wrote of his time and of himself. But what he had lived through, what he had seen, was, in his estimation, not only a historic event but an occurrence of timeless significance. What we are dealing with is not the threadbare cliché of "history repeats itself" but a mythic conception of history. In this context, the pronouncement: "Thus in human history there ever recur moments in which it threatens to come under the sway of demonic forces" is the key to Jünger's understanding of history. Or, to approach the issue from another angle: by negating the humanistic values, nihilism leads inexorably to the dominance of evil. Its utter destructiveness manifests itself in total conflagration.

Since the myth embodies the view of the cosmos embraced by men who are still closely tied to nature, it holds within it plant and animal as constituent elements. Thus the floral studies in which the brothers are engaged — and which afford us many glimpses of plant life — transcend scientific concern.

The brothers' abode is fittingly called "Rautenklause," that is, the hermitage around which the rue bushes *(Ruta graveolens)* abound. The special object of their inquiries is the lily, a flower whose record encompasses more than four thousand years, and whose venerable age is coupled with the almost global diffusion of some two and a half thousand species. Thus it is not by chance that divers and profound meanings attache to this flower. In Asian religions, the white lily *(Lilium candidum)* symbolizes light. It is sacred to the goddess Juno. For the Christian, it is a symbol of innocence and purity, as well as of grace and reincarnation. The fire lily *(Lilium corceum)* is thought to be the child of the sun and the earth; it symbolizes the victory of light over darkness. The gold-banded lily *(Lilium auratum),* which is native to "Cipangu" — the name which Marco Polo gave to Japan — grows in the garden of the hermitage; it is particularly dear to the brothers: "It will remain a marvel that such delicate forms of life are imbued with so great a power of love" (AM, 79). Since the lily is of august lineage, it is, for Jünger, the "member of a royal family, of a princely clan" (Str, 3, 427). And it is not coincidental that the gold-banded lily is in bloom when disaster is about to strike the land, when ineffable baseness is on the verge of gaining dominion. The lily is cause for reassurance and hope (which it also symbolizes): light will again prevail over darkness. A similar situation obtains when the brothers, following their successful search for the reed woodland orchid, happen upon the Chief Ranger's compound of wanton murder.

Not only the plant but the animal as well is central to intent and meaning of the novel. The greatest significance attaches to the snake: no other animal has engaged the mythic imagination so fully and ubiquitously.

The snake is widely held to be a godhead, the most august position it occupied in Yucatan: for the plumed serpent was the great god of the Mayas. Whereas, among the Incas, the snake occupies the nether realm guarding the underground treasures, it was thought to be the god of thunder among the Japanese. Since, owing to its shape, it is eminently a creature of the earth, it was accorded the power of fertility, indeed of cultural creativity, among the Guatemalans. There it was truly a creature of protean capacity; changing into different animals at will. Residing in heaven and in hell, it used its powers most ambiguously. In the Apocalypse, it is simply the devil. In the Graeco-Roman myth, the snake symbolizes fertility and is sacred to Minerva Hygeia, Athena, and Hermes. Aesculapius, the son of Apollo and the god of medicine, may be shown as a serpent. The caduceus, a winged staff with two serpents twined around it, is carried by Hermes but is also symbolic of the medical profession. Jünger himself refers to the serpent of Aesculapius as symbolizing the healing powers of the earth (see SK, 8, 74). He also refers to the custom of eating snakes, which was practiced in China and in Europe when a person's life was thought to be imperilled (see Str, 2, 419). Here is one of the most telling examples of the ambiguity of the myth: the serpent is endowed with both health-giving and death-dealing powers. The ambiguity is resolved when one remembers that these opposites — and even those that appear to be mutually exclusive — are of the mind's making only: life and death are but the two aspects of being. But the ways in which man reacts to the sight of the snake remain divers and contradictory. Fear, admiration, abhorrence, a magic spell — any one of these or a mixture of them may seize him. For Jünger, this is the "effect of the mystery revealed. Is it death? . . . Is it life? . . . Or is it something else, something more powerful from which both forces [life and death] break away like light and shadow, like positive and negative currents?" (Sat, 4, 309). As he elsewhere puts it,

It is the primordial power of these animals [snakes] that they embody life *and* death, as well as good and evil. At the moment when man — with the serpent's aid — gained the understanding of good and evil, he also gained death. This is why the sight of the snake is an experience of the most prodigious kind for everybody — almost more puissant than that of sex, with which it is also connected. (Str, 3, 101)

Although the snake is very much of the earth, and although its brain is minuscule, its mental powers are believed to be great and its wisdom extraordinary. The Bible knows the snake as wise but also as false and wicked, as treacherous and cruel. Among the Babylonians it was known as the incarnation of evil, but Jünger also calls to mind a gnostic sect, the Ophites, that is, the brethren of the serpent (Str, 2, 27). Its several groups were divided among themselves; some believed the snake to be a kind demon, while others thought it evil.

The fall of man exemplifies the serpent's divisive power. However, among African tribes, the snake is seen as encircling the earth, thus unifying its parts. The similarity to the Germanic myth is striking: the Serpent of Midgard holds the earth together with its coils. The circle that the snake forms by biting its tail is a ubiquitous symbol of continuity and immortality. Because it sheds its skin periodically, the snake is often believed to be immortal. One of Jünger's books, *Geheimnisse der Sprache* (Mysteries of Language), bears this symbol as its emblem in significantly modified form: the snake forms a double circle in the form of the mathematical sign for infinity (∞).

The serpent guards the august personage. Jünger refers to the pharaohs of Egypt (Sat, 4, 309), where Buta, their protector, was portrayed as a winged cobra. Conversely, the hero proves himself by killing the fearsome serpent. Hercules prevails over the nine-headed Hydra, and Perseus gains the head of Gorgo, "queen of serpents" (Sat, 4, 309).

Already in the account of his youthful African venture, Jünger refers to the snake as his "favorite animal." And from then on, his thinking centers on it again and again because he has come to see in it the animal at its most complete and in its perfection. He marveled at the snakes when he saw them glide through the water or rest in it:

All movements of these creatures are perfect; they produce great and simple configurations: the straight line, the circle, the oval, the figure 8, the letter S, the wavy line, and the ring whose beginning and end are intertwined. Such geometry is possible only because extremities such as wings, fins, hands, and feet are lacking. It is in this sense that the snake is not only the most perfect animal but is also animal most perfectly so: it embodies most perfectly the primal matter of life: the position most adequate to it is the horizontal one, when the body in its entire length touches the earth. (AF, 4, 143)

Not only the myth but also folklore or popular belief shape the role allotted to the snake in Jünger's novel. It is counted among the *lares domestici;* in the hour of need, it gives full account of itself as the guardian spirit of the hermitage. It is also shown as fond of women and children. The belief that the snake is partial to milk is very common, though scientifically unfounded. It responds to music, as the snake charmers insist; yet it cannot hear, it merely responds to their swaying motions. And the author also makes use of the belief that the coloration of the queen of serpents is different from, and more splendid than, that of her followers.

The conclusive proof that the snake is central to the idea of *Auf den Marmorklippen* — what it is and what it stands for — has been furnished by the author himself. He was about two months into his story when he noted: "The Queen of Serpents — I may perhaps come upon a better title, lest we be taken for ophites" (Str, 2, 27). Only two weeks later he wrote: "Queen of Serpents. I think I'll bestow a new title on this capriccio: 'On the Marble Cliffs.' It might even better convey my idea of the unity of beauty, grandeur, and danger" (Str, 2, 37).

This, then, is the manner in which a man who is, in the full sense of the word, at home among plant and animal, relates his myth-making to both of these realms. A similar relationship obtains between these realms and that of the dream, and inevitably, between dream and myth. Jünger exhorts:

Regard the animal as if it were a human, and consider man an animal quite its own. Think of life as a dream among a thousand dreams, and of every dream as a disclosure of what is real. (AH [1], 7, 128)

The dream discloses what is real, quintessentially real, because it rises from the nether reaches of the soul, from the unconscious, and is therefore neither strained nor distorted by the inhibiting power of reason or the superego. Since the unconscious is also the repository of the living past of the soul, it follows that myth and dream (and kindred phenomena such as vision, ecstasy, and hallucination) are of the same matrix. What we are here concerned with is dynamic psychology *(Tiefenpsychologie),* the findings of Freud and, especially, Jung and his followers, such as Kérenyi.

Jünger has spoken clearly of the impact of the irrational forces on the making of his book. I have already noted that he referred to it as a "capriccio," a term which, together with "Figur," he used for the subtitle to *Das abenteuerliche Herz* to characterize his particular kind of writing. "Capriccios," he explains, are "jestings, playful happenings of the night which one fondly watches as though seated in a loge of one's own. The sense is one of detachment yet, at the same time, of danger" (AH [2], 7, 181). This is the ambivalence of the "capriccio." What it relates is a dream or kindred experience.

Some thirty years after writing *Auf den Marmorklippen,* the author declared that the true quality of the story was "visionary" rather than "literary" (Ann, 477). Such a distinction is perhaps dubious; yet the intent is clear. The conscious fashioning of the story appears less important to him than its visionary core. He foresaw the great conflagration when the Third Reich — seemingly unchallenged — approached the acme of power.

The inner certainty needed for the writing of the *Marmorklippen* came to the author in a dream. He had equivocated when Hitler came to power. On the one hand, he refused to be quoted in the *Völkische Beobachter* and rejected membership in the nazified *Deutsche Akademie der Dichtung.* At the same time, he had declared himself ready to aid and support the "new state," but failed to carry out his intention. And then, less than a year before beginning to write

Auf den Marmorklippen, he had a dream while journeying in the Aegean:

Dreams give me hope for the future; they reassure me. This is particularly true of the dream I had while sailing for Rhodes, a dream in which I prevailed over Kniébolo [Jünger's pseudonym for Hitler] and his cohorts at the center of power. (Str*, 440)

However, the novel does not openly express this hope and reassurance; it only implies it.

The figure of the Chief Ranger is a clear instance of how the dream contributed materially to the novel. He actually came to the author in a dream in which, significantly, a snake played a crucial role. Jünger set down the nocturnal event in a "capriccio" entitled "Der Oberförster" (The Chief Ranger), which is included in *Das abenteuerliche Herz.* There is irony in this appellation, which suggests order and security — of the tyrannical kind. But Jünger saw the Chief Ranger also in the light of day; he therefore endowed him with prototypical traits borrowed from Bismarck, Stalin, and Hermann Göring.

It is worth noting that the characters of the novel bear unusual, often striking names. The protagonist's brother was originally named "Profundus." When the author found that the "triad" carried too heavy a phonic load within the sentence, he changed the name to "Felix," which he then rejected as too "colorless." He finally named him "Otho," which, he thought, readily fitted any phrase or clause (Str, 2, 43). The priest's name, Lampros ("the radiant one") clearly accords with the bearer's character. The brothers flee to Alta Plana to live with "Ansgar." Since he never enters into combat, we must assume that he is properly called "Ansgar," that is, "god's spear." The Chief Ranger's active adversary is Braquemart, a French word that means "cutlass" and also, in slang, "membrum virile." It is not clear how such an appellation fits the man, and the reference to the prototypes, Goebbels and Heydrich (the Gestapo chieftain), provides no clue either. And there remain the names whose significance cannot even be guessed at: Belovar, the herdsman; Lampus, the woman caretaker; as well as Erio and his mother Sylvia. However, a general observation suggests itself. The diversity of the names (Greek, German, French, etc. and the purely imaginary kind) is probably intentional: the author does not want the story understood in unequivocally geographical or historical terms.

To summarize the ways in which *Auf den Marmorklippen* partakes of the dream: an act of clarification and reassurance (the dream of Rhodes) is basic to the work, which ranges freely between the "wakeful" confines of time ("anachronism") and place (its "telescoped" quality). The protagonists often act with somnambulistic surety; and some of the events bear the hallmark of the nightmare: the discovery of the Chief Ranger's camp of iniquity, the nocturnal battle, particularly the encounter of dog and snake, and the fire consuming the land. And just as the dream is brief, so, too, is the story. No transitions are used to smooth the flow of events. The characters, though clearly drawn, are not subject to psychological development. There is neither a true ending nor a conclusive summation. As Jünger himself observed:

The book is open-ended, incomplete; the actual events are its continuation. They, in turn, play upon the book and thus also change it. In this sense, it resembles an ellipse: one of the focal points is held by the author, the other, by the events. Threads are being woven back and forth . . . (Str*, 79)

Auf den Marmorklippen does exemplify the surrealist position, the conviction obtaining that the true realities reside, and are alive, in the subconscious. This book is — in large measure — a gathering up of the yield of the *irratio,* of dream and vision.

CHAPTER 6

War, and The Peace

*A*UF *den Marmorklippen* had just been completed when the
Second World War broke out (September 1, 1939). Jünger
was called up and served, with the rank of captain, for the duration of
the conflict. Again he kept a diary which, in its published form, spans
nearly ten years, covering a period anterior to the war as well as three
years of the occupation (1945 - 1948).

This diary bears the title *Strahlungen.* The German word, in its
singular form *(Strahlung),* means both radiation and radiancy. It
denotes, as Jünger explains in the preface, the effect of the events on
the individual, that is, the author, or "the lattice work of light and
shadow" produced by them. Furthermore, it characterizes what
transpires between people, in close relationships as well as fleeting
encounters. These "Strahlungen" may serve, so the diarist hopes, to
enlighten the reader.

Comprising about nine hundred pages, *Strahlungen,* is Jünger's
most voluminous work. It is divided into six parts, the first of which,
Gärten und Strassen (Gardens and Highways), published under this
title in 1942, covers the period between April, 1939, and July, 1940.
The author had just moved from Überlingen on Lake Constance to
Kirchhorst, a village near Hannover, where he and his family occupied a former parsonage. He worked the large *garden* and pursued
his studies of plant life. The war came. Jünger first served as commanding officer of an infantry company. During the French campaign, his unit helped secure conquered territory, and he describes
the *highways* thus followed.

Parts Two and Four of the diary are both entitled "Pariser
Tagebuch" (Parisian Diary). Early in 1941, Jünger was transferred
to Paris to serve on the staff of the general commanding the German
occupation forces. His duties ended when, after the Allied invasion,
the staff was disbanded in August, 1944. Jünger's duties consisted in

making two studies. One of them was an analysis of a strategic plan
that was never carried out, "Operation Sea Lion," which embodied
the staff work preparatory to the invasion of the British Isles. The
other study involved the struggle between the Nazi party and the
military for supremacy in occupied France. As a routine task, he was
charged with censoring the mail of military personnel.

Part Three, "Kaukasische Aufzeichnungen" (Caucasian Record),
deals with a trip to the southern part of the Soviet Union, where the
German forces had just advanced to the Caucasus (October, 1942, to
February, 1943). This trip was made at the behest of the German
general Karl-Heinrich von Stülpnagel, who wanted an unvarnished
firsthand account of the Russian campaign. It was a crucial moment
because the debacle of Stalingrad was imminent. There was also a
political side to this mission. The general wanted to know whether —
and to what extent — the German officers corps on the Russian front
could be counted on in an attempt of the military to overthrow the
Hitler regime. Paris, it will be remembered, was the center of this
conspiracy, which led to the abortive attempt on Hitler's life on July
20, 1944.

Part Five of the diary "Kirchhorster Blätter" (Kirchhorst Journal), is the record of the last eight months of the war (August, 1944,
to April, 1945). The staff at Paris having been disbanded, Jünger was
ordered back to Germany to be discharged from the army. Although
not implicated in the July conspiracy, he was suspect because of his
close association with some of its leading participants. This is why he
was discharged from the service. Later on, however, he had to join
the *Volkssturm,* this *levée en masse* of youngsters and old men who
were called upon to offer final, desperate resistance to the Allies
moving into Germany. As the commanding officer of the Kirchhorst
district, Jünger prevented any such meaningless action. This part of
the diary ends with the day on which American armor entered the
village.

The "Parisian Diaries," the "Caucasian Record," and the
"Kirchhorst Journal" were jointly published in 1949 under the title
Strahlungen. Part Six of the diary, comprising the period of April,
1945, to December, 1948, is named *Jahre der Okkupation.* (It may
be noted that the author did not designate *Strahlungen* as the title for
all six diaries until 1962 - 1963, when they appeared as Volumes Two
and Three of his collected works.)

Jünger took part in two wars, but in strikingly different ways. We
remember the man who was singularly, indeed obsessively motivated

to prove himself as a fighting soldier. He was wounded seven times; he was awarded the highest distinction for exemplary valor. His diary, which recorded events and deeds, was made into a novel and two shorter narratives. Twenty years later, it was a radically different story. Jünger partook in the defense of a fortification that was never attacked. His only action consisted of helping to rescue a wounded soldier. For this he was awarded a medal, the lowest the army could bestow. Then followed security duties, staff work and an inspection of the Russian front. He was never promoted; and his discharge was barely honorable. Again, he kept a diary, but it recorded little, if anything, that could be turned into a fictional account. He rewrote his notes and elaborated upon them. Later editions of the diary were, as is his wont, revised (the "Parisian Diaries" and the "Caucasian Record" were shortened by one-sixth).

Keeping a diary, an age-old custom, generally does no more than serve the diarist's concern. But the time came when diaries were published, thus becoming a literary genre. For obvious reasons, those excelling in insight and style were composed by men of letters. Among these, to name but a few, are Samuel Pepys, Swift, Goethe, Friedrich Hebbel, Tolstoy, and Kafka. And then, toward the end of the last century, such records began to be published while the diarist was still living. The trend was established by the *Journal* of Jules and Edmond Goncourt (1887 f.). Men like Léon Bloy, Julien Green, Henri de Montherlant, and, notably Gide followed the example. And there is Jünger and, more recently, Max Frisch.

Whereas a literary work affords insight, in varying degrees and with varying success, into the author's temperament, character, and ideas, his diaries would seem to be testimonials that are direct and unequivocal. This may be true of those daily notations which were set down never to be published, or, if they were, only posthumously so. However, the living diarist who readies his notations for publication is constrained, again in varying degrees, by tact, by the consideration for living contemporaries on whom he comments, and by his reluctance, conscious or not, to speak freely of himself. But the ultimate (and well-nigh insuperable) difficulty is stated by Jünger: "What concerns us in our innermost defies communication, if not indeed our power of perception" (Str, 2, 284). Or: "We live in the dead angle of ourselves" (AH[2], 7, 290).

What, then, is the diary *Strahlungen* all about? Although it deals with the war years, these events, as we have seen, affected the author neither strongly nor dramatically. What the French campaign demanded of him is still recorded in some detail; of his staff work in Paris, only the bare facts of his assignments are divulged. Among his associates, and with some of his superiors (among them Colonel Hans Speidel, chief of staff to Field Marshal Erwin Rommel), the war was widely discussed. Yet what Jünger records of the several campaigns that concerned them most directly (Africa, Sicily, Italy, Southern France) is very limited and rather unilluminating. About the conspiracy against Hitler, there is more information. It will be discussed below, in connection with the tract *Der Friede* (The Peace).

Jünger also counted among his acquaintances a good many Frenchmen, excluding, of course, members of the *Résistance*. He associated with writers such as Pierre Drieu la Rochelle, who were sympathetic to the Nazi regime; and there are those who were seemingly "unengaged": Jean Giraudoux, Paul Léautaud, as well as Jean Cocteau, Marcel Jouhandeau, and Banine, the author of *Rencontres avec Ernst Jünger* (1951). He met Braque and Picasso, the latter telling him: "The two of us, as we are here sitting together, could negotiate the peace on this very afternoon. In the evening, people could turn on the lights" (Str, 2, 367).This was on July 22, 1942. Jünger also frequented the salon of Lady Orpington (pseudonym for Mrs. Frank Jay Gould). The conversations with Sacha Guitry, the famous actor, are described as lively; even the décor of the luncheon was thought worthy of recording: "The salad was served in a silver bowl, the ice cream on a salver of solid gold which had been owned by Sarah Bernhardt" (Str, 2, 274).

The social pastiche also included active collaborators. At the house of Paul Morand, the writer, then accredited as ambassador to Bucarest, Jünger met Benoist Méchin, a member of the Vichy cabinet, and Céline, who counted *Bagatelles sur un massacre* among his dubious books. He also knew de Brinon, ambassador to the Third Reich, who gave a luncheon, again a very sumptuous affair — guarded by twenty policemen (see Str, 2, 271). As the war went on and the tide turned, such social activities diminished. At any rate, Jünger had no qualms about attending them. He had stated long before: "For the writer, there is no such thing as bad company" ("Epigramme," 8, 653), which is to say that society, however dubious, is worth exploring.

Since his duties were apparently not very demanding, Jünger found much time for reading and visits to bookstores and the "bouquinistes" on the banks of the Seine. Among the books commanding his particular interest were those describing shipwrecks; he con-

sidered them instructive, symbolic of the times. But it is the Bible —
he read it for the first time in its entirety — which he most often
refers to and comments upon.

Gärten und Strassen contains an entry which, being brief and fac-
tual, attracted no attention at first. On March 29, 1940, his forty-
fifth birthday, Jünger noted: " . . . read the seventy-third psalm"
(Str, 2, 122). Eventually, it was remembered that in the Luther Bible
this psalm bears the caption "Tribulation and comfort of the pious at
the sight of the godless' good fortune." The psalm contains passages
castigating the unbelievers as "proud," "corrupt," and "violent":
about oppression they speak "loftily." They blaspheme the heavens,
and yet "their tongue walketh the earth." Though the ungodly
prosper, there is comfort. "Surely Thou didst set them in slippery
places: thou castedst them down in destruction." Finally: "For, lo,
they that are far from Thee shall perish. . . ." The latter-day
proponents of godlessness eventually demanded of the author that he
delete the reference to the psalm. He refused: and *Gärten und
Strassen* was banned.

Jünger read the Bible for religious as well as philosophical reasons.
He may have wanted to see if he could find a way of becoming a
believer, what role the Christian religion could or, indeed, must play
in postwar reconstruction, and how the ages are illumined by the
light of biblical verities.

Despite his metaphysical propensities, Jünger considered himself,
somewhat oddly, a "rationalist." As such, he felt compelled to prove
to himself, and rationally so, the existence of God. This entails a
struggle, reminiscent of Jacob's nocturnal encounter, in which God
shows Himself to exist and prevails (cf. Str, 3, 361). Jünger does not
say whether or not this attempted proof was successful. Looking
forward to what he will say (and not say) in later years, we may, at
best, surmise that the struggle continues. In his search, Jünger is
eminently the Protestant. Neither the community nor the church
proffer aid or support: "Of all the cathedrals, only one remains: the
one that folding hands build" (Str, 3, 213).

The diary also contains notations concerning a theology of history.
Representative of Jünger's train of thought is an entry which he
made at the height of the war, when the power of the Third Reich had
reached its acme. Referring to the first power struggle recorded in
the Old Testament, he writes:

Cainitic civilization epitomizes the civilization of pure power. Sodom,
Gomorrah, Babylon, Dahomey are late examples, after the Flood. Cainitic

also are the great *loci* of fratricidal festivals on this earth: The Mexican
theocalli, the Roman circus, the extermination camps of the machine age.
And Cainitic, too, are the red flags, regardless of the emblems they bear,
Hitler's SS, a battleship boasting the name of Marat. — Cainitic women are
described as exceedingly beautiful. *Dans l'état de la chute, la beauté est un
monstre.* (Léon Bloy). (Str, 3, 359)

(In the African kingdom of Dahomey, massive human sacrifices
were made to honor the deceased monarch. Brutal slave-raiding
campaigns were common. These practices endured well into the
nineteenth century. In ancient Mexico, the theocalli was a temple
where human sacrifice and cannibalism were practiced.)

This representative passage shows what Jünger finds in the Bible
that helps him understand history, notably the archetypal figures.
Cain, embodiment of "pure power," guides him through the ages and
allows him to identify similar figures and configurations. Historic
specificity pales in the light of what endures and recurs.

Power was also an immediate political issue. What was to be done
about Hitler, the latter-day Cain, who had established his regime and
was now conducting a war, both criminal and disastrous? A popular
uprising could not be counted upon because — and this is Jünger's
overriding argument — the people had been gruesomely victimized
and demoralized. There were, however, the military leaders, who had
the power and the opportunity to act. The "Fronde" within the German officers corps, numerically a small group, sought to enlist
elements of the high command. Jünger discounted the effort. Most
generals, he argued were "energetic but stupid." They had advanced
to their position because they carried out orders unquestioningly. To
this "capacity" debilitating senility must be added. Though there
were some enlightened generals, among them Karl-Heinrich von
Stülpnagel, his commanding officer, they lacked the will to act.
Rommel appeared to be the exception; he might lead or, at least,
cover the conspiracy. This hope faded when he suffered a disabling
automobile accident.

Jünger was also doubtful about the initial aim of the conspiracy:
the assassination of Hitler. He noted, after discussing it with Lieutenant Colonel Hofacker, one of the leading conspirators: "As I had
done before in other, similar instances, I expressed skepticism, dis-
trust, and also the dislike with which the prospect of assassination
fills me. Such action brings about but little change and, above all, no
improvement." Supporting his contention, he turns to the myth: "If
Kniébolo [his pseudonym for Hitler] falls, the Hydra will grow

another head" (Str, 3, 251; 298). One may counter by insisting that the Hydra grew seven new heads, yet Hercules succeeded in killing the monster, freeing man from the scourge. The assassination was attempted but failed. The diary records: "This was very instructive. The body cannot be healed while undergoing a crisis; the cure must apply to the whole body, not just a single organ. . . . Ours is a severe trial, fully substantiated and therefore necessary. Such wheels are not to be turned back" (Str, 3, 299). In other words: the historic event has a logic of its own; it is inevitable.

Jünger felt that if he could do his part, it would only be after the event had taken its course, after the war had been fought to its conclusive, bitter end. This contribution of Jünger's is a tract entitled *Der Friede: Ein Wort an die Jugend Europas — Ein Wort an die Jugend der Welt* (The Peace. An Appeal to the Youth of Europe — An Appeal to the Youth of the World), of which there are two versions. The first one was written between the winter of 1941 and the spring of the ensuing year. The author destroyed it a few months later; he has never accounted for that action. He only noted: "Its purpose [of writing *Der Friede*] was purely personal. It was to serve my own education — in the 'practice of justice,' as it were" (Str, 2, 18).

The second version was written between July and October, 1943. Its purpose had changed; it had become political. According to Benno Ziegler, Jünger's publisher, the programmatic tract was to appear after Germany had been defeated and had politically collapsed. It was to

influence decisively not only the political situation in Germany and the people's will regarding foreign affairs; it was also designed to give convincing expression of the political intentions of a new Germany. (*Der Friede.* Zurich: Die Arche, 1949, p. 86)

The manuscript was read by the author's associates and superior officers, among them Erwin Rommel, who also approved of it. In May, 1945, following the cessation of hostilities, *Der Friede* was to have been published. However, the Allied military government refused permission. Only four years later did the tract appear in print.

Der Friede consists of two parts. Whereas "Die Saat" (The Seed) expounds the governing philosophical ideas; "Die Frucht" (The Fruit) develops a political program. What are the "seeds of peace"? They are the sacrifices made by the adversaries in this global conflict. It has been a desperately fought war, understandable only to those who conceive of this war not as a trial of arms between peoples and states, between nations and races, but rather as a universal civil war which split the world into mysterious [and, therefore,] all the more terrible fronts. (DF, 24)

Untold sacrifices were also made by the civilian populations, the victims of total war. And further, there were the hapless inmates, incarcerated and killed, of camps of frightful notoriety. All this pain, suffering, and dying must not have been in vain. Jünger felt that he was also among the victims, for his eldest son was killed in action.

The seed can only grow, and eventually bear fruit if the war ends decisively, in Germany's utter defeat. An enduring peace cannot be built on compromise. But such peace is possible because the victorious and the vanquished will come to realize that, all differences notwithstanding, they live in a world that has become as one: the war has been the great equalizer.

The program for peace, though concerned with Europe alone, may nonetheless serve as a guideline for the rest of the world. Territorial reorganization is imperative because Europe is, in fact, a "geographical unit." This will make it possible to integrate the Continent economically, which is also one of the ways of preventing future wars. The freedom and the dignity of the individual must be legally secured and a constitution promulgated from which all laws derive.

Whereas the constituent nations of a unified Europe will enjoy complete cultural freedom, "uniformity of organization [is indicated] in whatever concerns technical matters, industry, commerce, communications, trade, weights and measures, and defense." Jünger's argument that "the forms [that is, the methods] of the authoritarian state apply where men and things can be organized technically" is highly questionable (DF, 60). In an authoritarian state, the governing agency is answerable only to itself; it is neither compelled to, nor does it, account for its actions. Jünger evidently believed that the European government he envisaged would be composed of men who exercise unrestricted power in "technical matters" in a responsible manner.

The "Arbeiter" was again to play a leading role: he was to demonstrate that he was endowed not only with soldierly virtues but with constructive talents as well:

The peace will have achieved its aims when the forces which are given over to total   mobilization are freed for creation. Then the heroic age of the "Arbeiter" will have reached its fulfillment — the age which was also the age of revolutions . . . the "Gestalt des Arbeiters," losing its titanic cast, will reveal new aspects of itself — then it will be seen what relation it bears to tradition, creation, happiness and religion. (DF, 57)

Religion lends ultimate emphasis to the tract. If world peace is to be achieved, it must be based on, and secured by, a "sacred compact." Jünger forsees developments akin to a worldwide religious rebirth:

> . . . in spite of all tribunals and treaties we will plunge deeper into destruction if the transformation remains purely humanitarian and is not accompanied by a theological one. Yet there is hope of great changes. For instance, the Russian revolution stands on the brink of developing new phenomena, and there are many indications that, having begun as a technical and political transformation, it will find its final accomplishment in metaphysics. (DF, 63)

Nihilism must be overcome. In countering debilitating thought and destructive action, religion must play a decisive role:

> . . . the danger has become so great that each one of us must be asked . . . to make a confession of faith. We have reached a point where, if not belief, at least piety, an effort to live justly in the highest sense of the word, can be demanded of mankind. (DF, 67)

He who swears only by man and human wisdom must not, as judge, pass sentence; must not, as teacher, guide; must not, as physician, cure.

Theology must be restored to the rank of *prima scientia*. Religion and state can no longer be separated; the church must be sanctioned by the worldly power. In Europe, it will be unified. The century-old schism will be overcome because the trend toward unity is universal. Jünger even argued that the general constitution must be synodal in nature.

Though he deleted the statement from later editions, Jünger noted in the war diary: "As to perceiving historic realities, I am ahead of the times, that is, I perceive them earlier, before they become manifest" (Str*, 407). In this instance at least, such capacity failed him. Certain it is that *Der Friede* raises more questions than it answers. Why did the author limit his appeal to the young people (subtitle of the tract!) as they could not be instrumental in refashioning the world? How can democratic and authoritarian methods be reconciled? What are the signs pointing to religious rebirth and ecumenical unity? Would the Soviet Union and her allies be responsive to such a program? Even in the West, a positive response would have been less than likely. And as questions are raised, they mount.

In sum: *Der Friede* is a mind-boggling document.

CHAPTER 7

Heliopolis

A UF den Marmorklippen and *Der Friede* notwithstanding, Jünger was politically suspect: his activities as *National-revolutionär* and his book *Der Arbeiter* had not been forgotten. The Allied Military Government, therefore, subjected him to the denazification process, demanding that he fill out the standard questionnaire relating to a subject's political past. Jünger refused to comply; he insisted that he had not been a National Socialist, let alone a member of the party, and that he was therefore not liable to be investigated. The authorities rejected his argument, and since he persisted, forbade him to publish, a verdict that was not lifted until 1949.

In spite of this proscription, the four years following the war were very productive. Two books on travels he had made in the early 1930's, and an essay on the symbolism of language (*Sprache und Körperbau.*), were published in Switzerland — beyond the pale of the verdict. Four parts of *Strahlungen,* the war diary, were readied for publication. They appeared, together with a full-length novel, in 1949.

This novel is *Heliopolis: Rückblick auf eine Stadt* (H. Looking Back Upon a City). It is Jünger's most ambitious epic work, comprehensive (the original version comprises 440 pages) and complex as to intent and content. The author therefore felt that he should help the reader understand what he had tried to accomplish.

Jünger holds that a novel worthy of that designation must be "autark" (self-sufficient): "The reader lands on it as on an island, finding there everything he needs. This betokens the author's freedom, his sovereignty. In the manner of a lord, he leads the reader on-to his domain." "Island" means the novelist's world. If he deals with it comprehensively and fully, the reader is capable of understanding and appreciating it unaided.

The novel must also be "universal," that is, "it must relate to the world as a whole." This is not, and patently cannot be, a question of spatial comprehensiveness, "since 'the whole' may be seen in a farmer's room as well as a royal palace. The 'whole,' the effect it creates, is rather a matter of atmosphere: one realizes that persons, things and places are embedded in the cosmos." The world is presented not in material fullness but in the form of a "model." Heliopolis, a city, is conceived as such a model. The literary effort results in a "Weltroman" (world or universal novel).

It follows that the novelist must not restrict himself to any particular topic or approach. Psychology, "Bildung," society, religion, history (among others) are *aspects* of the novel, but any or all of these have a rightful place in it.

Jünger further insists that the novel must be neither "realistic" nor "idealistic," since approaches such as these preclude the presentation of "the whole":

In this sense, there is no such thing as a naturalistic, a romantic, or a documentary novel ["Tatsachenroman"]. On the other hand, there is, and has always been, the classical novel, if one conceives as classical man's sovereign intent to envisage the order of things inherent in the whole. The universal novel ["Weltroman"], which epitomizes this intent, excludes all time-bound particularities and thus becomes meaningful for all nations and all times. (H, 10, 401 - 402; In the course of a revision, the excursus on the novel was eliminated from the text and transferred to an appendix.)

Jünger does not say what exemplary novels he has in mind, but it would seem that, for one, Goethe's *Wilhelm Meister* is a case in point.

Heliopolis is the imaginary *locus* of events. It has nothing to do with the ancient Egyptian city, the capital of the realm named after the sun god, or with Baalbek, the Assyrian metropolis, which was also dedicated to the solar deity. The name Heliopolis is merely allusive; as the author presents a timeless prototype of the city, not a historical realization of it. Campanella's *Città del Sole* may also suggest itself, but it is a utopia, whereas *Heliopolis* merely holds out hope for the rebuilding of the true order of human affairs, a hope based on the idea of the cyclical recurrence of events.

The time of the action is the future, yet the extent of this projection remains vague. The author speaks of the era "after the second nihilism," from which it may be inferred that the globally constituted "Arbeiterstaat" has come and gone. The present situation may be described as an interregnum since a precarious balance of power has been established. The Proconsul, supported by the army, represents the forces of conservatism. He is opposed by the Governor (Landvogt), a ruthless authoritarian who holds sway over the masses. The third contending party are the Mauritanians, a small but closely knit order. They are the nihilistic "technicians of power" who seek to exploit the standoff of the major factions. *Auf den Marmorklippen* comes to mind, for the Governor is akin to the Chief Ranger and the secret order is called Mauritania in both novels.

Since there are no subplots, the events center solely on the protagonist, who is Lucius de Geer, a man perhaps in his early thirties and very accomplished indeed. He is a man of action, a diplomat, and an officer of great skill. Since he is also highly cultured, his company is welcomed by artist, scientist, and philosopher alike; with them he converses on an equal footing. Being handsome of mind and body, he is attractive to women. Ultimately, Lucius de Geer is an embodiment of the "adventurous heart." There is no risk he will not take, and by running risks, whether succeeding or failing, he accomplishes a remarkable self-realization. His name symbolizes what and who he is. "Lucius," deriving from "lux," signifies striving for light, for spiritual enlightenment. The "de" shows that he is an aristocrat, both by birth and of mind and character. The word "Geer" means lance or spear; it stands for the protagonist's soldierly and chivalric virtues. His coat of arms is the point of a spear shaped like a lily. What this flower symbolizes has been shown already in the chapters *"Das abenteuerliche Herz"* and *"Auf den Marmorklippen."* (The protagonist's surname may have suggested itself to the author by Baron Karl de Geer [1720 - 1758], a disciple of Linné's and an entomologist like him.)

Concerning the plot of the novel, three aspects may be distinguished. De Geer acts as teacher, diplomat, and soldier. He is being associated with a variegated group of men; his discussions with them satisfy his artistic, scientific, and philosophical interests. And there are the encounters which involve him psychologically.

De Geer, the outstanding soldier, aware of the ethics of his profession, is charged with conducting a class at the military academy, which is designed to develop the student's sense of moral responsibility — a demanding task in view of the prevailing conflict which may flare up in civil war — the kind of war that is most ruthlessly fought. Yet de Geer insists that an officer must never be an instrument or a mere agent. For him the soldier is a man of conscience lest he betray the profession. The Chief of Staff, de Geer's immediate superior, fears that such an uncompromising view will detrimentally affect the students' attitude. There is no meeting of the minds. De Geer realizes that he has failed, that, perhaps, he could not have but failed.

Although this is not a time of open hostilities, acts of terror are committed from time to time. Thus the Governor's chief of police is assassinated. Although it is not clear who committed this particular act, the Mauritanians are suspected. However, the Proconsul, anticipating accusations and protests, asks de Geer to offer expressions of "sympathy" to the Governor on his behalf. The latter exceeds his mission by asking for, and obtaining, the release of Budur Peri, the daughter of an acquaintance of his. She is a Parsee, belonging to a persecuted minority against which the Governor has aroused the populace. Following her release, she joins de Geer's household. He has succeeded as a humanitarian but failed in his diplomatic mission because the Governor now holds information compromising the Proconsul's faction.

The time comes when the Governor is to be reminded of the Proconsul's strength and willingness to act. A commando raid is organized to destroy the "Toxicological Institute" which, victimizing members of the persecuted minority, engages in inhuman experiments — similar to those carried out in concentration camps. De Geer is in charge of the successful raid but, instead of following the clear order to blow up the Institute, he first searches it to rescue any living victims of the toxicological experiments. He finds one, Antonio Peri, Budur's father. But precious time has been lost; the commandos are almost caught while withdrawing. De Geer, once again, has almost failed by obeying the dictates of his conscience.

This is all that "happens" in the novel. By contrast, the protagonist's associations with a fully representative group of men, the exposition of their ideas, his response to, and reflections on, them, fill out most of the novel's framework.

De Geer's closest acquintances are Halder, the painter, Ortner, the poet, and Serner, the philosopher. They meet regularly to discuss, in the manner of a symposium, aesthetic and philosophical questions. The protagonist participates, demonstrating that he is not only a man of action but also, and eminently so, a man of parts. One of the symposia is fully recorded; it is devoted to the problem of happiness. What we read is actually an essay in diologue form, a device which allows the author to expound the various facets of the issue in the dialectic manner, as live, dramatic expressions of several points of view. The conversation is supplemented by Ortner's reading of a novella he has just completed. A man meets a latter-day Mephistopheles who poses as an ophthalmologist. He couches his victim's cataract, that is to say, he makes him *see* what goes on — in other people's minds. By dint of such "insight," he gains great power and wealth. But since all his enterprises inevitably succeed, his fate is ennui and unhappiness. Thus the question of happiness is being dealt with in the abstract and in the form of a parabolic tale.

One of de Geer's acquaintances is Orelli, a historian who tells of Lacertosa, an (imaginary) island whose cultural remains he has studied. He stands for the true scholar, the man who is thoroughly conversant with the facts but also endowed with sensitivity and intuitive insight. This enables him to envision the true nature of this ancient civilization. And he also masters the word; his account is that of a poet. The ultimate meaning and import of this account — as well as that of the symposium on happiness — is suggested later on in the novel:

This is the situation that allows us to aim at happiness. It is clear that it must be enjoyed by all, and fully so. The earth must be rounded, become a closed living space. It is a favorable sign, that the planet has assumed the character of an island. Let us remember that the islands are the ancient abodes of happiness. (H, 10, 193)

In Orelli, the protagonist recognizes the true historian: the philosopher in command of the facts and endowed with the power of the poetic word. He is, in A. W. Schlegel's words, a "rückwärtsgewandter Prophet" (a prophet looking backwards).

De Geer also learns about the earth and its origins. It is the *Bergrat,* a philosophically inclined geologist, who tells him of the (imaginary) "Turres somniorum." They are said to be located in the Caucasus, a region on which geological and cosmological speculations often center:

. . . a gray, opaline dusk prevails. Mortal man who wends his way through this ring of crystalline monoliths reflects on their origin in vain; the scientific mind does not penetrate such depths. However, one may presume that elements infinitely superior to the kinds of fire known to us have been at work here. Those fiery elements have risen from below, the core of the earth, or descended from above, from outer space. In the remote past, at a glorious

hour, these cosmic jewels glowed in sevenfold splendor, at the edge of creation, in constellations never to be understood. Here, at the sight of these
towers, one realizes that the great cosmogonies and the myths of the world's
creation are infinitely truer than all scientific chimeras. (H, 10, 23)

The *Bergrat* practices what Novalis called "verkehrte Astrologie"
(astrology in reverse). In a "Weltroman" such as *Heliopolis,* a model
of the mineral world has its place, just as Orelli's account of Lacertosa embodies the realm of history.

    Both Orelli and the *Bergrat* are mystagogues who clarify and ar-
ticulate de Geer's view of the timeless verities that are contained in
the myth. Lacertosa and the Turres Somniorum are shown to him as
what they are: indestructible, ever-recurring patterns of civilization
on the one hand, and of the physical cosmos on the other. Their views
are supplemented and enriched by Father Foelix, a figure represen-
ting the world of the divine, who lives at some distance from
Heliopolis, in the Pagos. (The word denotes the rural areas surrounding the city.) Such a locale is indispensable to the "Weltroman,"
since man's world comprises both country and city, nature and
civilization. His hermitage is open to all those seeking spiritual guidance. He also keeps bees, and thus the novel of cosmic scope is made
to include another realm, the animal kingdom. Having reflected on
the apian community, Father Foelix has come to oppose the view of
its being soulless, hierarchically controlled, and driven to labor un-
ceasingly. He rather thinks that theirs is a community worthy of
emulation.

The apiary could serve as a model for the states of man, if one wants to consider it to be a state — as a model if one envisions, as the goal to be attained,
the raising of the political order to the level of relationships governed by pure
love. This you find in the ancient kingdoms by the grace of God, but also in a
true democracy. However, the question of a constitution is of no import. . . .
The best constitution is of no value if brotherly love is lacking.

From the apian community to the Gospel is but one step:

Christ has taught us about a community based on love, and this he showed
by the way he lived. *Imitatio Christi* is, above all, the mission of the Church;
for this reason, it will remain indispensable, to complement and exalt
worldly authority. Admittedly, this great goal — as is true of all true goals
— is unattainable. But it must remain the lode star lest man be lost in
darkness. (Hel, 246)

Although the author struck this passage from the final version of the novel, he did not mean to disown these ideas. Already in his earliest writings (see the chapter "Eros" in *Der Kampf als inneres Erlebnis*), he conceived of love as a cosmic force, counterbalancing the powers of destruction. The cosmic conflict may also be understood as the battle between Ormazd and Ahriman, between light and darkness, because Jünger holds that the pagan myth and the Christian religion do not exclude but confirm each other.

Whereas his various associates have helped de Geer to see and learn, it is Father Foelix who has — in the literal sense of the word — enlightened him:

Lucius felt — and it was an experience he shared with others — that he could not maintain his rigid ways in the Father's presence. His mind touched him like rays that melt ice. He opened up the heart, infusing it with new life. It was an irruption which, like the realization of a great love, was exceedingly painful *and* fruitful. The superhuman aspiration, the idol which de Geer had erected in himself, began to totter. Light struck it down. (Hel, 299)

Father Foelix made de Geer see what love is: a cosmic reality and a religious force. He must still experience it as the power that binds together. Only by being bound in love, he becomes fully himself.

Budur Peri is the only female character Jünger has ever developed; she is a remarkable, most complex figure. In this respect, she is the counterpart to Lucius de Geer. She represents the East and the West: her father is a Parsee, a member of the Indic sect of Zoroastrian persuasion, while her mother was an occidental "of the North." Budur is an educated woman with the curiosity of the "adventurous heart"; her mind is akin to de Geer's. The name is symbolically significant. According to Persian tradition, Peri is either an evil female spirit or, more generally and equivocally, a supernatural being of either sex. The latter meaning is suggested here. De Geer's companion is eminently feminine but endowed with the mind of a man. She holds her own in deeply probing discussions with him. Budur denotes "full moon." Generally, the moon is represented as a goddess (Ishtar, Artemis, etc.), the lunar cycle being thought to symbolize the female, particularly the maternal, principle. Beyond this, Budur Peri proves herself to be the lover incarnate, suggesting not only Artemis but also Aphrodite.

Budur and Lucius engage in wide-ranging conversations in the course of which they become increasingly aware of their affinities, which binds them ever more firmly together. However, what they have in common is not only ideas but also that curiosity which reaches beyond the limits of the conscious mind. Together, they venture into the dark realm of the soul by ingesting hashish. During this voyage into the unknown, they realize beyond all doubt that they are kindred souls, for the drug they share opens up the same vistas.

The drug-induced dream transports them to a site of intense, ceaseless activity. Human corpses, dismembered and rotting, are unloaded, piled up, reloaded, and carted away. The output of liquidation camps is collected here, probably to be distributed to plants which extract from such remains what is economically usable. The sign "Distribution Point No. 23 — Section No. 1" indicates that this is a far-flung, thoroughly organized operation. The "distribution point" is called "a senseless perpetuum mobile in its basest form" (Hel, 398), also "the ghastly kitchen of the world of the Titans" (H, 10, 325). These embody mighty forces which seek to destroy the divinely ordained order of things; in the present context, they stand for the powers of brutally antihuman nihilism whose rule had just come to an end when *Heliopolis* was being written. They have risen again — the novel is projected into the future — and have done so with increased ruthlessness. Whereas at Auschwitz the victims were gassed and cremated, nothing is wasted here; even the corpses are fully "utilized."

De Geer is overpowered and despairs at the sight of the horrendous spectacle. "Nothingness ["das Nichts"] has conquered him, displaying fearsome power and exhibiting great joy; it has entered him as though he were a fortress to which it had laid siege for a long time" (H, 10, 326). Yet the trial is not over. To view another "perpetuum mobile," he is urged on into a city, where the people are frantically active. Work is performed in the manner of slaves or of robots; the pleasures exalt violence and depravity. It is all pain and suffering, intensely felt by de Geer.

He breaks down at the sight of nihilism, of destruction which is inflicted upon man and which he inflicts upon himself. On the conscious level, he knows what nihilism is and opposes it. He succumbs as he now realizes that, without his knowing, it has been contained in him. The drug, the key to what his innermost holds, has afforded him this insight into himself. This is his condition, but not his alone. Dostoevski had asked: "From where do the nihilists come?" And he had answered: "They come from nowhere, for they are always with us, within us and about us."

The newly gained awareness that the nihilist is also "in" him shatters de Geer. But he can regain hold of himself because Budur Peri is at his side, sustaining him with her love, which is also that of the self-denying mother. (She is the embodiment of the archetype also in this regard.) Until he met her, he had been self-centered in his erotic relationships. What he had sought in them was metaphysical satisfaction. "As a supernatural lover, it had been his wont to see through, to see beyond his partner, directing his view at the absolute — as through a magic glass fashioned by Aphrodite." But now "love had hit him like a bullet, making a mockery of his heraldic device ["de ger trift" — the spear hits the target]. For the first time he understood that he needed a human being, a very special one, to be sure" (Hel, 413).

This is the consummation of de Geer's "education." Paradoxically, he was "educated," came into his own, by failing — as a diplomat, as a teacher, and as an adventurer of the spirit. What restores him is love.

Where does he go from here? He cannot remain in Heliopolis, because a man such as he, a man of uncompromising views, will, through his actions, compromise others as well as himself. But his time may yet come. This is the Regent's view, who, having withdrawn to a regal residence in the stratosphere and waiting watchfully, invites de Geer to join his entourage. The emissary tells him: "We know your situation. It is that of the conservative who has failed in his attempt to employ revolutionary means" (Hel, 432). What his function will be remains unsaid. At any rate, the time is not ripe yet for the Regent's return, for a monarchical order built on religious foundations, for an order "where power and love are in accord. . . . The solution depends on a new conception of the word *father"* (Hel, 426). De Geer accepts the invitation. Accompanied by Budur Peri — whom Father Foelix has joined to him in wedlock, he makes his departure in the Regent's spaceship. Mention was made of a "residence in the stratosphere" and of the "spaceship" as a means of transportation. Since *Heliopolis* is also a "Zukunftstroman," it anticipates technological advances. Computer and data bank have been fully developed. Combination transmitters and receivers have been adapted to individual needs and reduced to pocket size. The weapons systems have reached a high degree of sophistication (death rays). Not only the stratosphere but also Antarctica have become habitable. With the exception of the data bank ("Haus der Briefe" [House of Letters]), the technological innovations are not described.

Since they are only referred to as fact, they are not elements of science fiction but are designed to serve the idea of the "Zukunfts-roman."

A novel which purports to fashion a model of the world ("Weltro-man") is a complex enterprise. The plot of *Heliopolis* may be simple, but speculation abounds. A view of the future can only be speculative. For this reason, *Heliopolis* is, ultimately, a philosophical novel because the author's true concern is not the phenomenon, but to show what

> . . . . binds
> The world together, so that I'll find
> the forces stirring at the core . . .
> (Dass ich erkenne, was die Welt
> Im Innersten zusammenhält,
> Schau' alle Wirkungskraft und Samen . . .) (Faust I)

It is in this sense that *Heliopolis* offers a view of the world — not only a most personal view but also a comprehensive one. Jünger's novel does indeed embody a *summa scientia,* a summation of what the author had done, thought, and written about. All this material could not be properly integrated. As a result, the work contained much that was fictionally irrelevant and therefore aesthetically injurious. This is probably the reason why the author revised it radically, shortening it by about one-third. *Heliopolis* is now a better book, but the original version is more interesting and more illuminating because Jünger not only set down what he thought but also commented on it. From the aesthetic point of view, this was a questionable procedure. Earlier, he had said: "He who comments on himself lowers his standards" ("Wer sich selbst kommentiert, geht unter sein Niveau") ("Epigramme," 8, 654). In revising *Heliopolis,* he took this admonition to heart.

CHAPTER 8

In Quest of the World

JÜNGER is probably the most widely traveled man in the history of German letters. He once said: "We would be true citizens of the world if the earth, the earth as a whole, had formed and fashioned us" (Str, 2, 455). In his own way, he has endeavored to live up to this conviction. This may seem paradoxical since he is intensely German, in certain ways irritatingly so. However, Germany was never his sole, narrow concern. The lands, the continents beyond, always beckoned. Youthful impulse drove him to seek the wonders of the Dark Continent; enlisting in the French Foreign Legion was but the means to this end. The scope of *Der Arbeiter* is not narrowly German but encompasses the globe. *Auf den Marmorklippen* was intended to show that the German events were of wide, typical significance, that they transcended the fate of a particular country. And the object of *Der Friede* was global reconstruction.

Jünger began his travels in the 1920's, and the *Fernensehnsucht* (desire to see distant lands) is still strong in the man approaching the age of eighty. What attracted and fascinated him earlier was the Mediterranean: the sea, the lands along its shore, the islands. Northern Europe also beckoned; in his later years he reached ultima Thule. Gradually, the circles widened, touching the Americas. Voyages to Africa and Asia Minor followed. Eventually he set out for the Far East.

Surely, Jünger is a man of his days, of his times; but his view also embraces the past. He is, therefore, ever eager to sharpen his sense of history. It is, in particular, the points of significant contact to which he finds his way: Dalmatia, to which the Ottoman Empire extended its rule and influence in Europe; Rhodes, the Western outpost facing Asia Minor; Sicily, where Normans and Saracens once held sway. But these regions are also depositories of earlier civilizations, those of ancient Greece and Rome. And it is their great myths in which Jünger finds inspiration and support for his views.

The past comes alive, and so does what enduringly renews itself: nature. Jünger is an amazingly knowledgeable and keen-eyed naturalist who is at home among plant and animal in the subtropics of the Mediterranean, in the South American and Asian tropical forests, in the temperate as well as in the arctic zone. He is a botanist of note, a competent ichthyologist, and above all, an impassioned entomologist:

> The study of insects has consumed an unconscionable amount of my time. Yet one must see this as a tilt-yard where one practices the art of subtle discernment. It affords insight into the most delicate features of a particular region. After forty years one reads the texts of the teguments in the manner of a Chinaman who knows a hundred thousand ideograms. (Str, 2, 487)

Jünger wrote this passage at the age of forty-seven. Already as a child he had begun his study of insects. Eventually, he gained professional competence: three insects, first identified by him, bear his name.

Jünger is indeed a very perceptive traveler. He knows, and knows about, what he is going to see, and since he is equipped with sharp and trained eyes, he sees more, is prepared for the unexpected, the fortuitous. His are the benefits of serendipity.

What he has seen, and his reflections upon it, have been set down in thirteen travel books. Impressive record though this is, it is by no means complete because he has not written about all his travels. The form of his deposition varies: for the most part, Jünger uses the diary, but, on occasion, he chooses the letter or the straight narrative to record his experiences.

It is a striking fact that most of his travel books — no fewer than ten — describe voyages to various islands: Korcula (off the Dalmatian coast), Sicily, Rhodes, Sardinia (and adjacent islands), Corsica, the Canary Islands, Ceylon, Formosa, and the Japanese islands.

Jünger has frequently shown why islands attract him, why they fascinate him, and what they mean to him. Thus he meditates upon approaching the Cape Verde Islands:

> When I see the islands rise up and disappear from sight, I am always overcome by intense nostalgia — I always feel as though I had lived in ancient times where the cliffs solemnly tower in the sea. Delicate threads attach the

soul to the promontories enshrouded in clouds, the entrance gates to marvelous valleys. They break when the island fades away in the mist.

Spell-bound by the ocean, we feel as if we were released, dissolved; everything that is rhythm in us comes alive: suggestive sounds, chords, melodies, the primal song of life [*Urgesang des Lebens*] resound across the times.

By contrast, the islands hold the promise of profound happiness, of quiet, of peace — in the midst of the deeply agitated, tempestuous elements. (AF, 4, 169)

His speculations describe ever wider circles: "Everything is island, even the continents; and the earth is an islet in an ocean, the ether" (SP, 4, 335). "Life is like a green island in the dark sea of death" (Str, 2, 364). "In the void, God created an island: the universe" (H, 10, 116).

The sea, in which the islands are embedded, holds mysteries of equal depth. Jünger describes the experience he had on San Pietro, off Sardinia:

I swam from a ledge over to the left, into an enshadowed bay. Here another, a mythic sea, opened up, the cliffs being nordic, Ossianic, melancholy and mysterious. The entrance to a grotto rose high like the ogives of a cathedral. The plaintive cries of large marine birds hovering above the dark vault sounded prophetic. A sunbeam penetrated the solemn twilight, striking the pale pinions, which whirled like snowflakes before the dark portal.

I saw the grotto from the water flowing through the bay, surging and sucking, yet barely rippling the surface. I had the feeling that a sea monster, half sleeping, half waking, was plying its tentacles upon my body. I could tell its stirrings by the blond crowns of the seaweed swaying below. . . . The water was magnetic as though here the mass of the sea had been compressed. In our days, the physicists have shown that there is such a thing as heavy water, but it has been known since time immemorial that, in his boundless realm, Poseidon possesses grottoes, palaces, and playgrounds which he visits with his retinue to find pleasure. There the water not only refreshes and heals but is also imbued with divine virtues. (SP, 4, 356)

This passage suggests a comparison with what impressed Jünger at the mountainous shores of Norway. (He had traveled there in 1935. The record, in epistolary form, is entitled *Myrdun* [1943].)

These mountain ranges are somehow unquiet, like formations that are not yet completed. One inclines to believe that their ridges still drip with the waters from which they have emerged. Particularly where, in the form of extended peninsulas, they are joined to the sea, they appear shaped like powerful, long-necked lizards, whose flanks, shining with the deep golden green of

the forest, are covered with soft, resplendent skin. Sailing by them, one holds
his breath, for the gravity of the rock inside them presses upon the heart like
a heavy shadow. What would it take (and it would not be much) to rouse one
of these monsters from its sleep? (Myr, 4, 85)

Not only the eye but other senses as well may come into play. Having taken a solitary walk near Antibes, Jünger writes:

When the wind blows, everything becomes an instrument. When, as at this
hour, the sun shines and we close our eyes, the sense of well-being springs not
only from fragrance and warmth but also from the voices of animals and
even from the stirrings of that world which we call inanimate, and which now
begins to assert itself joyously. This is an orchestra now joined by the sand of
the dunes and the pebbles of the seashore, as well as the rustling of the
bulrushes. . . . The universe lives . . . soft crackling like thoughts astir: pine
cones whose scales are rising up.
  These are the sounds of nature. At times, it seems as if the world with all
its mysteries were contained in them. . . . The great philosophical pursuit
begins where physics and metaphysics are separated by no more than the
thinnest of films. (Ant, 4, 423)

Jünger is also a dedicated student of plant life. This, as well as his
entomological, interest he developed as a boy, since his parents lived
for the most part in small towns: garden and countryside were the
ambience in which he grew up. For the last forty years (interrupted
only by the war) he has lived similarly. Taking frequent walks and
cultivating a garden have remained integral to his life. It is therefore
not surprising that his writings, the diaries in particular, abound with
observations on plant life and, as is his wont, meditations upon it. In
the passage that follows, he describes the subtropical luxuriance of
the Canary Islands:

Walking through a grove of chestnut trees, I came upon a farm enveloped in
rainy mist; it was like the treasure house of everlasting spring. Tropical, subtropical, and central European plants grew side by side, blooming and bearing fruit. Bushes resplendent with oranges, shrubs hung with pomegranates,
fig trees and Japanese medlars crowded among banana trees. The purple of
roses emulated the scarlet of the "burning bush," a large euphorbia, aflame
with efflorescences ("Scheinblüten"). Potatoes and peas were in bloom at the
foot of a hedge of prickly pear. It was covered with vines in wax-colored
bloom. Bougainvilleas, creeping high, fairly smothered the house, and it was
almost a miracle that the walls were equal to this burden of colors.
  The remoteness and the peace of the place contrasted felicitously with the

excessive manifestation of *vis vitalis*. One imagines Aeolos' island in like manner: peaceful and calm, though it is the appointed abode of the storms. Here I gained an idea of the palette on which Spring mixes its colors — to be spread over countries and empires. Godlike peace and serenity enveloped this spot. (AF, 4, 175)

Jünger's ability to describe and convey impressions becomes clear by the way in which he juxtaposes them. Having taken a walk across the Norwegian moor, he writes:

Even before we stepped out of the forest, the clusters of cottongrass showed that the moor was near. This plant, which favors the spots where peat crops up, is here known as myrdun, that is, moordown. Its inflorescences are thought to be distaffs from which elfins spin their yarn and weave garments for their kings. The Norwegians greatly love the moor, so much so that, in poetic parlance, the sea is named "blue moor." This region is perhaps characteristic of their mode of living, of a life of scant abundance, of an economy at the edge of wilderness. Up here, the extent of the moor is clearly apparent: one can walk for days without seeing a soul. The colors are delicately monotonous; no painter has yet discovered them. Green and gray are interwoven, radiating yellow and silver shadings. In spots, the water reaches the surfaces; then brownish black, spongy banks emerge from green cushions. Here and there trees drowned by the flooding of the roots. The elements have completely stripped them of their bark, reduced them to shiny skeletons; the woodpeckers work away at them. A hidden beauty pervades this region, which saddens, but also gladdens, the heart. There is much of this in the Nordic sagas. He who is ignorant of this beauty does not really appreciate their mood. (Myr, 4, 79)

And this is how a single plant impressed itself upon him while he was walking near Antibes on the French Riviera:

Yet another plant always makes me linger, a strange one, which spreads a green cover of feltlike leaves over the hot crushed rock: Momordica. It is related to squash and pumpkin, produces, simultaneously, countless yellow flowers and prickly fruits shaped like tiny melons. As they mature, they become explosive. When touched, they open up with the report of a child's pistol and emit amniotic liquor and seeds. One such discharge hit me in the face; the taste was bitter, puckering the mouth. Late in the season, one need only walk through such a growth to be shot at by something reminiscent of the artillery in *Gulliver's Travels*. (Ant, 4, 412)

With equal dedication, impassioned and empathic, Jünger observes the splendor and mystery of the animal world. Here he describes an encounter in the Brazilian forest:

As I was standing before a papilionacea, its pistil protruding like a lion's tongue, a small animal came flying near. I thought it was a bumble bee until I realized, joyous and amazed, that it was a bird, a humming bird. The plumage was russet, the color of cinnamon; the eyeline was long and brown. While it was hovering before the blossom, the tail was turned toward the body, spread like an elegant fan. The beak, a lightly bent foil, stabbed into the calyx. Then it flew off like a spark, perched on the dead branch of a large tree. There it tarried, no more than a line or the stem of a leaf. (AF, 4, 131)

The Sardinian coast is dotted with ancient watchtowers commanding the sea. The guards alerted the islanders when the ships manned with Arabs, intent upon predatory invasion, approached. Jünger calls them "Sarazenentürme," towers of the Saracens. In one of them, he observed a nesting falcon:

Now and then we peer through this embrasure into the workshop of the universe, at one of its creations. The sight of such a heraldic animal yields the immediate certainty that power is one of the keys to its understanding. But as every color demands its complement, so power, an entity also, reveals its meaning by something else. How shall one name this "something else"? Perhaps beauty, or love? I would call it happiness. If power is the male principle of the universe, then happiness is its female counterpart. Without the latter, which complements and balances, power may become very ugly as we have witnessed in our days. As power is the key, so happiness is something to be unlocked, an inexhaustible treasure lying at the bottom of the universe. The appearance of an animal such as this falcon confirms this fact; we feel that it is not only magnificent but that it must also be happy, must have access to the entire, undivided reality of the world. Therefore, it bears the marks of this condition: it is beautiful, strong — strong also in love, as on the first day of creation. (Sat, 4, 280)

On observing the scarab, the scatophagous insect, at work, Jünger meditates:

Why did the Egyptians count it among the sacred animals? Its mode of life may be said to be saintly because, less destructive than even the vegetarian, it feeds on the excrements of the herbivores and, in so doing, cleans up their grounds. And then there is its manner of breeding: embedding the ovum in a ball of excrement which it buries. This must have engendered deep thoughts in the minds of a people dedicated to the cult of the mummy and the grave. So it was natural that they related the scarab's ways to burial, resurrection, and to the rising and setting sun. And, indeed, this winged animal was represented as holding the solar disc with its forelegs. (Sat, 4, 269)

Jünger's relationship to the animal is very close, at times acquiring mystical intensity:

This is one of the exquisite pleasures which consciousness can grant us: we penetrate the very depth, the depth of the dream which is life, and live with the animal, and in it. It is as though a tiny spark had darted over to us, a spark of the extraordinary, unreflected joy that animates it. (Str, 3, 29)

Although Jünger has also visited countries where the traveler's focus is, in the main, the cultural heritage (Greece and Italy in particular), he has preferred to record voyages which afforded him contact with nature, which allowed him to broaden his knowledge of, his insight into, the worlds of mineral, plant, and animal. Man interests him, and almost exclusively so, in relation to his natural habitat. Even when he describes a cultural phenomenon, an artistic creation, his interest is aroused by the way it relates to its surroundings. Here he describes the Doric temple of Segesta in northwestern Sicily:

With the land around it, the temple has entered into a union of unfettered power and harmony. The day was gloomy and windy; the moving clouds and the firmly balanced mountains seemed governed by this shrine. If it did not stand there, the forces of nature would engage in battle, in the manner of the Titans. The ideal relationship of power and harmony has been accomplished by a structure balancing, harmonizing the dimensions, the vertical with the horizontal.

Buildings like these are power plants of the highest order; in their sphere, heroes and the muses throve for centuries. Such temples are, on the one hand, embodiments of chthonic forces, that is, the soil is crystallized in them. Being also creations of the mind, they manifest both unconscious and conscious power.

Making my way up to the amphitheater, I often looked back upon the temple. It is to their great credit that the Greeks knew the quality, the rank of reduction and its relationship to size, as indeed the crystal strikes us as a model of the earth. Scaled down in size, the model reveals all the more clearly what it represents. — The state was the patron of the arts, yet regarding architecture, it performed, it created. Splendid buildings directly reflect the political order. In them it could have exhibited its greatness in the manner of the Cyclops; instead, it created sublimated models that blend power and art. (GM, 4, 96)

The description of Nikko, the "Mecca of Japan," permits a striking comparison:

The extensive, magnificent woods were dedicated to worship; they abound with pagodas, temples, mausolea, bronze columns, and statues. Today it is called "The National Park." However, in Sanbutu-do, its largest shrine, the "three divine manifestations" are still being worshipped: a richly gilded seated Buddha; Kwannon [deity of mercy] on thrones of lotus, horse-headed on the right, with a thousand arms on the left; and statues of twelve disciples rise in the background. Everywhere, resplendent among deciduous trees and evergreens, religious edifices. Built of wood, they are lacquered red and adorned with intarsias. Such is the five-storied pagoda, donated about 1650 by Tadakkatsu, a feudal lord. When it burned down, his family had it rebuilt. It rises in the grove of cedars. Had we not seen it, we could not imagine its strange, baffling beauty even in our dreams. It embodies a singular conception of statics, also a musicality quite its own. Pure verticality is apparently insufficient; it, therefore, is balanced and harmonized by designs that reach out horizontally. . . . The wind combs its roofs; clusters of bells cajole it into playing upon them. Such chimes also adorn the bronze column. (LI, 47)

CHAPTER 9

Gläserne Bienen

GLÄSERNE Bienen (The Glass Bees), a short novel, was published in 1957. It deals with an apian insect that is made of glass and performs by means of a built-in mechanism and remote control. Yet the novel does not exemplify genuine science fiction because the device is neither described nor explained, nor is a new cinematic technique which is also mentioned. The device and the innovation merely serve as means of probing trends and consequences, the very meaning of technology. Like *Auf den Marmorklippen* and *Heliopolis, Gläserne Bienen* is essentially a philosophical novel.

The plot is a simple one. Captain Richard, a retired army officer, has fallen on hard times. A friend, through whose good offices he seeks employment, recommends him to the great Zapparoni, an industrial magnate in the field of automation. An interview for a position involving plant security is made. Surprisingly, Zapparoni conducts it himself in his splendid, sumptuously furnished residence. He puts the candidate to a twofold test. By posing a complex problem, he wants to measure the Captain's power of ready judgment. Zapparoni is clearly dissatisfied because the responses he receives are slow as well as equivocal. However, instead of being dismissed, the Captain is asked to take a walk in the adjoining park while Zapparoni attends to urgent business. Innocuous as this invitation appears to be, it turns out to involve the second part of the test.

The park is magnificent. It is summertime, the flowers are in bloom, the bees at work. But the realization is inescapable that these insects are not apian creatures but automatons made of glass, perfectly performing under invisible directions. The hives are also made of glass, receptacles into which the "bees" discharge the nectar which is artificially transformed into honey. Yet a still a greater surprise is in store for Captain Richard. On a pond, strange objects are floating. They are cut-off human ears — a frightening sight until the shocked observer notices that they are replicas, deceptive in their perfection.

The Captain is at the end of his wits. Angry that he has failed in the interview, upset over the flying automatons, and scandalized by those floating objects (he had retrieved one to inspect it closely), he compulsively vents his feelings. With a golf club found in a pavilion, he swings at and destroys "Smoky Gray," a rather large flying automaton, probably a controlling and news-transmitting satellite. At this point, Zapparoni makes his carefully timed appearance. He upbraids the Captain, regretfully rather than angrily, for the rash action. However, an amicable conversation ensues in the course of which he surprises the Captain by offering him a position, that of chairman of a "court of arbitration," which resolves disagreements among the board of planners and inventors. Zapparoni is satisfied that here is the man suited for a position which calls for "a sharp eye for technical matters" and "the power of discrimination" (GB, 147). The Captain accepts the offer.

Gläserne Bienen is a slender novel, and small indeed is the number of its characters. Twinnings, the helpful friend and intermediary, briefly appears at the beginning to get the story going. But only two figures are actually involved in it: Captain Richard and Zapparoni, who radically differ by virtue of character and position.

Jünger has always been intrigued by the likes of Captain Richard: the chivalric soldier who cannot adjust to warfare governed by the machine; the "adventurous heart" driven to engage in parlous enterprises; the moralist angered because the true, that is, his, values are discredited; the outsider rejecting, and rejected by, society; the man seeking, but failing to find, "solutions." The Captain is aware that he is a "mass of useless and antiquated prejudices" (GB, 12); his is a sense of frustration and defeat. Considering this condition, his name is sheer irony: Richard means "hard ruler."

His career is recounted by means of flashbacks. He dedicated his life to the army. Upon being commissioned, he was appointed to the cavalry — there was no doubt in his mind that this was the noblest branch of the service. He was privileged indeed because "the great, the godlike union with the animal" (GB, 89) was vouchsafed to him. But the days of the mounted soldier were drawing to a close; the horse had been replaced by the tank. So he did most of his fighting, in two global conflicts and in "Asturia" (obviously a reference to the Spanish Civil War), from inside one of these armored vehicles, which he despised but to which he nonetheless had adjusted. He developed a degree of technical competence that led to his appointment as "instructor at the tank-inspecting station." Yet this was a dead end, the end of his career, because his superiors considered him " 'an outsider with defeatist inclinations' " and rated him as " 'unsuited for positions of leadership' " (GB, 58-59). Captain Richard accepts this evaluation, but he also knows that it is too narrow. His problem is basic: he is an anachronism, a living fossil. His world is no more; his is a time of radical, violent change, the direction of which he cannot discern.

The Captain sees himself as "suspended in mid-air" — a metaphor derived from a pathetic occurrence. As he recalls his past, his comrades in arms pass in review. Among them there is Lorenz, who, at odds with himself and the times, has tried to recover ground to stand on by returning to "nature," by embracing the primitivistic socialism preached by Tolstoy. His attempt at acquiring certainty was, of course, futile. In a fit of desperation he jumped out of a window, to his death, while his friends, the Captain among them, watched horrorstruck. We also hear of Wittgrewe, another classmate: a splendid personality endowed with all the talents demanded of the outstanding officer. But the wars that are fought in this age offended his sensibilities and his ideals. He took his discharge to live a life of undisturbed and undisturbing mediocrity: he became a streetcar conductor and married a woman of apparently engaging simplicity. Twinnings also retired from the service; he adjusted by establishing some sort of employment agency which specialized in furnishing unusual services (including the dubious kind).

But there is one classmate whose military career has been a success. Weathering all storms, social and political, equal to all vicissitudes and changes, and making the best of adversity — he would not know what "perturbation" means — Field Marshall Fillmor has ascended the ladder to the topmost rung. Captain Richard is not impressed by his "briskly disposing intelligence, by a man who merely serves as a conduit of power": "In our day, a successful general, a high commander on the winning side, stands the best chance of becoming top dog in industry or politics. This is one of the paradoxes of an age that is unfavorably disposed toward the soldier" (GB, 77). The one officer of whom he not only approved but whom he also admired was Monteron, his teacher at the academy. Having died on the field of battle, he was spared tribulation and disappointment.

(The ideal preceptor is a recurrent figure in Jünger's writings. Their names are of the same derivation: Nigromontanus *[Das abenteuerliche Herz]*, Schwarzenberg *[Besuch auf Godenholm]*, and Monteron in this instance. The mountain is, of course, a complex symbol; the meaning that applies here is "loftiness of spirit.")

Considering the scope of the novel, this full passing in review of former associates is perhaps not wholly justified aesthetically; but, by dint of comparison and contrast, it serves the purpose of establishing the protagonist's character.

This is the Captain's dilemma: he is an officer "sicklied o'er with the pale cast of thought," the man of action who can no longer act in his appointed capacity. Supported by a study of history, he has concluded that the time is irreparably "out of joint," that this is an era of global civil war ("Weltbürgerkrieg"). (The translators' rendering of this term as "universal war" [p. 55] is misleading.) As a result, he has become skeptical and incapable of partisanship. Summing up his predicament, he observes: "My defeatism reached a climax: Totally affected, I finally turned my back on the struggle for power. It all seemed meaningless and futile, a wasted effort, time lost" (GB, 59).

Giacomo Zapparoni, whose father had "crossed the Alps, penniless and on foot," has risen to a station of great wealth and power. He is the manufacturer of "robots of every imaginable purpose," his specialty being the Lilliputian kind. His first inventions were

tiny turtles — he called them "selectors" — which were designed for picking and choosing. They could count, weigh, sort gems or paper money and, while doing so, eliminate counterfeits. The principle involved was soon extended; they worked in dangerous locations, handling explosives, dangerous viruses, and even radioactive materials. Swarms of selectors could not only detect the faintest smell of smoke but could also extinguish a fire at an early stage; others repaired defective wiring, and still others fed upon filth and became indispensable in all jobs where cleanliness was essential. (GB, 6)

He has also applied the idea of the robot to the making of toys, since he has understood that the element of play (*Spiel*) is inherent in this technical device. Clearly, "gadget" and toy are often one and the same thing. Finally, he has turned to making moving pictures, replacing the actor by life-size and lifelike robots.

This man is not only a technological genius, a tycoon amassing wealth and power, but also a man interested in matters of the creative mind. His is a splendid library; and the paintings adorning its walls bespeak exquisite taste.

Although Zapparoni is old and of slight stature, Captain Richard is impressed:

> Vor allem die Augen waren von grosser Kraft. Sie hatten den Königsblick, den weiten Schnitt, der oberund unterhalb der Iris das Weisse sehen lässt. Der Eindruck war zugleich ein wenig künstlich, wie durch eine feine Operation hervorgebracht. Südländische Starre kam hinzu. Es war das Auge eines grossen blauen Papageien, der hundert Jahre zählt. Das war kein Blau des Himmels, kein Blau des Meeres, kein Blau der Steine — es war ein synthetisches Blau, das an sehr fernen Orten von einem Meister, der die Natur übertreffen wollte, erdacht worden war. Es blitzte am Rand der Vorweltströme, beim Flug über die Lichtungen. Zuweilen schoss aus dem Gefieder ein grelles Rot, ein unerhörtes Gelb hervor.
>
> Das Auge dieses blauen Papageien war bernsteinfarben; es zeigte, wenn er ins Licht blickte, die Tönung des gelben und im Schatten die des braunroten Bernsteins mit uralten Einschlüssen. Das Auge hatte grosse Begattungen geschaut in Reichen, in denen die Zeugungskraft noch nicht vereinzelt ist, wo Land und Meer sich mischen und Felsen phallisch am Delta aufragen. Es war kalt und hart wie gelber Karneol geblieben, von Liebe unberührt. Nur wo es in den Schatten blickte, dunkelte es wie Sammet. Die Nickhaut zuckte darüber hin. Auch der Schnabel war hart und scharf geblieben, obwohl er über hundert Jahre lang diamantharte Nüsse geknackt hatte. Da gab es kein Problem, das nicht gelöst wurde. Das Auge und die Probleme — sie waren wie Schloss und Schlüssel aufeinander angelegt. Der Blick schnitt wie eine Klinge aus federndem Stahl. (*Gläserne Bienen,* 9, 433)

Above all, his eyes were extremely strong. They had the royal look, the open gaze, revealing the white of the eyeball above and beneath the iris. The impression one gained was at the same time slightly artificial, as if it had resulted from some delicate operation. Moreover, the eye had a fixed stare, peculiar to people of southern countries. It was the eye of a big, blue, century-old parrot, with the nictitating membrane twitching over it. This was not the blue of the sky, nor the blue of the sea, nor the blue of precious stones — it was a synthetic blue, produced in remote places by a master artist who wished to excel nature. Such a bird had flashed on the edge of primeval streams and flown over the clearings. Sometimes a shrill red and a fabulous yellow darted out of its plumage.

The iris of its eye was the color of amber; exposed to the light, it showed a tinge of yellow, while in the shadow it looked brownish-red with age-old inserts. This eye had seen enormous copulations in realms where procreative power is not yet individualized, where land and sea intermix and phallic rocks loom up at the delta. It had remained cold and hard like yellow cornelian, untouched by love. Only when it looked into the shadow did it become dark and velvety. The beak, too, had remained hard and sharp, although it had cracked nuts, hard as diamonds, for more than a hundred years. Not a single problem remained unsolved. The eye and the problems — they fitted one into the other like lock and key. His look cut like a blade of flexible steel.(GB, 62/63)

This is an astounding feat of description, the appearance of the great Zapparoni being unimpressive in all respects except one. It is his eyes that are remarkable; and only through them does he come alive. They are described as both human and avian. Zapparoni's character is equally impressive:

. . . he combined power and insight, acquired cunning and innate dignity. What was his heraldic beast? A fox, or lion, or one of the large predatory birds? I [Captain Richard] rather imagined it to be a chimera, like those which roost on our cathedrals and look down on the town with a knowing smile. (GB, 61)

He rules over his business empire with autocratic might, but, es-chewing public appearances, he has, through the manipulations of his public relations agency, created of himself an image of beneficence, that of a Santa Claus.

Captain Richard is clearly puzzled:

Did he [Zapparoni] want to dominate man, to paralyze him, or to lead him into fabulous realms? Was automation, in his eyes, a gigantic experiment, a test to be passed, a question to be answered? I thought him capable of theoretical, even theological reflections; I had seen his library and looked into his eyes. (GB, 71)

Gläserne Bienen embodies a philosophy of technology, Jünger's own, which is presented as the Captain's thoughts while he is waiting in the library and also while being exposed to the "calculated capric-cio" (GB, 145) in Zapparoni's park. The Captain regards the era which has culminated in his lifetime as that of the "dynamite civilization" (GB, 68). It began with the invention of gunpowder, the utilization of which called for the rifle and ever more potent devices (cannon, etc.). With the invention of the combustion engine, technology came into being, and eventually into its own. War became increasingly destructive and extensive, being total as well as universal. Ferocity reached its height when the struggle for supremacy also came to involve conflicting ideologies, when the op-posing powers engaged in global civil war. But even when put to peacetime use, the machine maims and cripples:

The brutal exhibition of severed ears had shocked me [Captain Richard]. But it was inevitable as a sign. Wasn't it the necessary result of the perfection of technology to whose initial intoxication it had put an end? Had there been, at any period in the history of the world, as many mutilated bodies, as many severed limbs as in ours? (GB, 112)

However, the glass bee appears to be a positive achievement. In this small robot, performing the function of an animal, perfection has been attained. It represents a triumph over nature because this bee, as well as its hive, performs with utmost efficiency. It extracts the nectar fully but does not aid in pollination, in perpetuating the flower. The little robot therefore serves to show that technology, as it reaches perfection, exhibits ever more clearly its destructive character: it exploits but does not replenish, ravages but does not repair, and exhausts beyond recovery:

Bees are not merely workers in a honey factory. Ignoring their self-sufficiency for a moment, their work — far beyond its tangible utility — plays an important part in the cosmic plan. As messengers of love, their duty is to pollinate, to fertilize the flowers. But Zapparoni's glass collectives, as far as I could see, ruthlessly sucked the flowers dry and ravished them. Wherever they crowded out the old colonies, a bad harvest, a failure of crops, and, ultimately, a desert were bound to follow. After a series of extensive raids, there would no longer be flowers or honey, and the true bees would become extinct in the way of whales and horses. Thus the goose would be killed which laid the golden eggs; the tree felled from which the apples were plucked. (GB, 98)

The author here alludes to Father Foelix (*Heliopolis*), the keeper of bees, who is aware of the "cosmic plan" and performs in harmony with it. By contrast, Zapparoni is a most dubious apiarist who nefariously interferes with the natural order of things. But, being the great inventor that he is — could he not improve on his bee so that it would also pollinate and fertilize, serve as "messenger" of love?

Zapparoni is shown not only as a technological genius, a man who knows how "to invent the inventors" (GB, 63), but also as possessed of "musische Neigungen," of being deeply interested in the arts. He has created a new type of moving picture — another technological triumph — in which life-size robots have replaced the actors. The Captain has seen a recent production and is impressed by this version of "Romeo and Juliet":

I am not, of course, going to maintain that they excelled human beings — that would be absurd after all I have said about horses and riders. On the other hand, I think that they set man a new standard. Once upon a time, statues and paintings influenced not only fashion but man. I am convinced that Botticelli created a new race and that Greek tragedy enhanced the human body. That Zapparoni attempted something similar with his automatons demonstrated that he rose far above technology, using its means as an artist to create works of art. . . . Here the world of marionettes became very powerful and developed a subtle, carefully reasoned-out play of its own. The marionettes became human and stepped into life. Leaps, drolleries, caprices — which only rarely had been thought of before — now became possible (GB, 137, 138)

Though the novel ends here, the reader may look forward to a continuation: "Soon perhaps, I [Captain Richard] shall describe in detail the consequences which my position as an arbitrator entailed, my experiences within Zapparoni's domain" (GB, 148). This continuation has not been forthcoming. Instead, the author added an epilogue (not included in the English version) when, in slightly revising the text, he prepared *Gläserne Bienen* for inclusion in his collected works. In this epilogue, an unnamed student of history reports on a seminar which a Department of Biography conducts on "Problems of the World of Automation." The current series, with Captain Richard in charge, is named "Transition to Perfection."

It is not indicated how much time has elapsed since the interview, how the Captain has fared in Zapparoni's employ, and whether or not he still serves as "arbitrator." To find him in his present role is perhaps not surprising because he has been described as a student of history. At any rate, the reporting student, while critical of the seminar as a whole, is pleased with the Captain's preceptorial performance. Although he does not offer "solutions," insisting, rather, that the facts must speak for themselves, he does not lack a historical sense. He is convinced that the events are governed by inner necessity, that their course is inexorable and that, all appearances to the contrary notwithstanding, history is meaningful. The historians, least of all the specialists among them, are incapable of extracting meaning from the events. Only the poet, the man possessed of intuitive insight and the creative word, can suggest what history, the ultimate order of things, is all about. The epilogue (it comprises no more than four pages) offers no more than generalities of this kind.

Although one should not demand of a short novel more than it can give, *Gläserne Bienen* has its flaws. The Captain's past, particularly his associations, command an inordinate amount of space. By contrast, Giacomo Zapparoni remains, for the most part, shrouded in mystery. We are asked to believe (but are not *shown*), that he is a tycoon *and* a benefactor of mankind, a businessman with the reputation of Santa Claus, Mephistophelean but also kind. He is a sorcerer, a *homo ludens* playing extraordinary games. Both characters, the Captain as well as Zapparoni, are burdened, perhaps overburdened, with ideas — those of the author. What appears to be a novel or, rather, the opening chapter of one, is, in the main, an essay in narrative form, an essay on automation and its creative possibilities.

CHAPTER 10

Toward a New Age

IN *Der Arbeiter* (1932), Jünger had set out to show that a new age in the history of man was at hand. Though the statement was extensive, it was groping and incomplete. He therefore thought of "revising" it, of doing this "thoroughly," or even of writing an altogether "new version" (DA, 6, 12). None of these plans were carried out. Instead, he wrote *An der Zeitmauer* (1959). Literally translated, the title reads *By the Wall of Time*. The word "Zeitmauer" is analogous to "Schallmauer," that is, sonic barrier. Breaking through that barrier was a technological feat and Jünger believes that he has also accomplished a momentous breakthrough which opens up a new vista. It can now be seen that the revolutionary changes of our time do not affect only man, his way of thinking, his values, and his institutions, but the earth itself. Our approach must, therefore, change; the historical perspective is too limited and must be replaced by a cosmological view of things. Consequently, the "Arbeiter" is not only the agent of man but of the earth itself. Metageological (or "geosophical") speculations are central to *An der Zeitmauer*. In short, it is a book which treats of man within the cosmic framework — an attempt that must employ an appropriate concept of time.

An der Zeitmauer is a long essay. The preface is entitled "Fremde Vögel" (Strange Birds). It is followed by an opening statement: "Messbare und Schicksalszeit: Gedanken eines Nichtastrologen zur Astrologie" (Measurable Time and Time Incident to Fate: Thoughts of a Non-Astrologer Concerning Astrology). The body of the essay, also superscribed "An der Zeitmauer," is divided into three parts: (1.) "Humane Einteilungen" (Human Divisions); (2.) "Siderische Einteilungen" (Sidereal Divisions); and (3.) "Urgrund und Person" (Cosmic Matrix and the Individual).

The preface "Fremde Vögel" sets the tone of the essay. In it, the author tells of two birds, the waxwing and the bee eater, which, being rarely observed in Germany, are "strange" phenomena. The scientist explains that unusual climatological conditions in their natural habitat prompts their occasional appearance elsewhere, in a region equally favorable to survival. However, the unusual event may be a matter of deep concern. According to popular belief, both waxwing and bee eater are birds of ill omen. The waxwing is actually called "Pestvogel," a bird that presages the outbreak of the plague. The scientist, conversant with the climatological facts, could have foretold the uncommon appearance of this bird (and perhaps did so), but his is a scientifically supported prediction — in contrast to the inexplicable avian prophecy.

Jünger then turns to a contemporary incident. At the beginning of the year — it was 1958 when he began to write the essay — he noticed an unusual interest in astrology. This suggested to him a widespread feeling that fateful events of great scope were in the making. Not only man but the whole cosmos was involved in revolutionary changes.

Although he insists that he does not believe in astrology, that he does not accept its "findings" ("thoughts of a nonastrologer"), Jünger nonetheless considers its presuppositions and basic concepts capable of providing guidance. Although man is of the earth, the framework of his being is the cosmos. If he wants to understand what he is and what he is going to be, he must disembarrass himself of his geocentricity and embrace a cosmic view of things. His evolution and history cannot be understood in the narrow terms of progression in time but must involve wide cycles of cosmic occurrence. And although time, taken as a quantity, may be measured, its qualitative aspect is of ultimate significance. Every hour, every day, every year is of equal, measurable duration; however, they also have a quality of their own. The stellar constellation determines the individual's fate but also that of larger entities, such as a city or a people:

To hear that his actions, his labors and encounters mean something more than he has assumed, that in them great powers assert themselves and endow them with meaning — to perceive this is clearly man's ineradicable concern. (Z, 6, 423)

Astrology flourishes in times of uncertainty, of crisis. And even though the feeling that a catastrophe is imminent may be widespread, Jünger holds that the great upheaval in which man and his earth are involved is not cataclysmic.

The first chapter of the main part of *An der Zeitmauer* bears the title "Humane Einteilungen." It essentially deals with history, our views of it, and the concepts underlying our understanding of human events.

Jünger is convinced that history is meaningful. By way of example, he cites Hegel, who had interpreted history as the unfolding or progressive realization of a spiritual entitity which he called the "Weltgeist" (universal spirit). Comprehensive though this view may appear, it is limited because it fails to take into account man as a creature of the earth, as chthonically bound and active. To understand this fact, it must be remembered that "history" is a relatively modern concept. Herodotus (*ca. 500 B.C.*) is generally spoken of as the "father of history." Before him, it was the myth by means of which man had tried to understand himself in a thoroughly comprehensive manner: who and what he was individually and collectively, in relation to the earth and to the gods. The mythic view is indeed cosmic in scope. When Herodotus speaks of the myth, he uses the terms "night" or "darkness" to show that a radically different age is at hand: the age of "light," the dawn which he perceived.

Jünger now feels compelled to ask:

Is "light" too of limited duration? Is this a turning point, perhaps even more significant than that of Herodotus' time? Are events no longer connected in the manner which we call historical, but in a different way, which has not yet been named? (Z, 6, 476)

And he elaborates:

Herodotus looked back from the dawn of history into the night of the myth, when the radiant light fell even upon the gods. There is a historical Jesus but no historical Jupiter. Ours is history at midnight; the last hour has come; we are looking into a darkness in which the things to come show their contours. The view fills us with dread, with weighty forebodings. It is an hour of death but also of birth. The things we see or seem to see have as yet no name, are nameless. (Z, 6, 481)

The great change is imminent because man is ready for it:

It is in our innermost that the Pillars of Hercules must fall before the New Hesperides come into view. [The ancient Greeks thought of the Pillars of

Hercules (Straits of Gibraltar) as delimiting the western reaches of the world known to them. Beyond lay the Hesperides, a paradisiacal island suggesting the Golden Age.] More questions arise. There are many indications that leaving the age of "history" will be more incisive, more fateful than leaving the age of the myth. This allows us to surmise that a far larger cycle has been completed. Might man not be called upon to sacrifice, to leave behind, more than he did then — in the end, humanity itself? (Z, 6, 490)

However, this final question does not suggest or imply that man faces a wholly destructive catastrophe but rather that the traditional concept of humanity must be radically revised. In a manner of speaking, man may "die," but he will be "reborn."

The question now poses itself for Jünger: wherein lies the momentous significance, the fatefulness of this turning point in the events of man and the earth? Jünger holds that the present, the highly advanced stage of technological development, allows us to see what is involved. Technology must be understood as "Form und Ansatz einer neuen Erdvergeistigung am Abschluss der historischen Zeit" (Z, 6, 502), as the "form and beginning of a new spiritualization of the earth in the closing stage of historical time." Man is engaged in harnessing the forces inherent in the earth. In penetrating the very essence of matter and gaining full control over it, he has become capable of performing literally earthshaking tasks. However, Jünger's views, though scientifically sound or relevant (nuclear fission and what it involves), must be understood as metaphysical. He conceives of the earth as an entity endowed with will, which, from time to time, man, its obedient and ingenious son, is called upon to carry out. It is once again the myth, as will be shown later, that inspires and supports Jünger's thinking.

As far as the scheme of events is concerned, Jünger's basic concept is the triad: (1) age of the myth; (2) age of "history"; and (3) the new age (as yet unnamed). It is well to remember that the triadic concept of history pervades Western thought. Typical examples include the division of the ages into that of the Father, the Son, and the Holy Spirit, suggested by Joachim of Floris (d. 1202). Gotthold Ephraim Lessing posited these phases as those of the Old Testament, the New Testament, and a third gospel, according to which man's action would be governed not by fear of punishment (O.T.) or by the hope of achieving eternal life (N.T.) but by the quest for moral perfection as an end sufficient unto itself. Hegel's scheme comprehends the universal spirit ("Weltgeist") as an abstract reality and its becoming manifest in nature and history respectively. With Marx, on the other hand, the concept is strictly historical: "Urkommunismus" (primal or primitive communism) is antithetically followed by the age of privately owned means of production, which will be replaced by fully developed communism.

The second chapter of the main part of *An der Zeitmauer* is entitled "Siderische Einteilungen" (Sidereal Divisions). The word "sidereal" derives from "sidus," Latin for "stellar constellation." Jünger's thinking proceeds from the basic fact that the earth is not sufficient unto itself, is a planet, a star among stars and thus an integral part of the cosmos. The history of man must, therefore, be delineated and understood within the cosmic framework. And this is precisely what the great cosmogonies (Old Testament, Greek and Nordic myths, etc.) accomplish. Their general scheme of thought is the triad: creation — destruction — rejuvenation or renewal. Jünger considers the widespread feeling that a catastrophe is imminent highly significant. This feeling obtains because man now has it within his power to thoroughly ravage the earth. This, he agrees, is possible but is not likely to happen. He rather thinks that the general dread is symptomatic of a strong, but generally inarticulate, feeling that an age is drawing to a close and a new one is about to begin, that changes are occurring which involve not only man but also the earth itself. Simply put: these changes will be both historical and geological. It requires seismographic sensitivity to discern this fact. Goethe possessed it — in the literal sense of word — when he predicted the earthquake which shook Messina on November 13, 1823. The disastrous eruption of Mont Pelé in the Caribbean (1902) led Léon Bloy — a writer whom Jünger regards highly and often quotes — to observe that this event was the first visible link in a chain of unexpected phenomena. This is the kind of seismography which links the geological with the human (or historical) event, the volcanic eruption being but a part of a general upheaval.

Modern man not only studies the earth (geology) but also fashions it. Jünger refers to such activities as deforestation, irrigation of arid regions, changing the prairie into arable land, strip mining, reclaiming land from the sea, and the like. It is, however, highly questionable that these activities lead to creating a new geological stratum. The changes involved appear to be — contrary to Jünger's view — merely topographical. At any rate, this is the thrust of his argument:

The meaning of the earth is beginning to change. An end which also signifies a new beginning ["Einschnitt"] has a tremendous impact on that stratum on which man lives on this earth. It affects every individual, every people, the cultural conditions of countries as remote as Tibet. The geological structure is also changing, a change which man brings about as agent (subject) as well as instrument (object).

From a vantage point like this, the great revolutionary changes within and among nations are but symptoms of a general restlessness which affects the very foundations of our being. These changes concern man as such rather than his institutions, since they tend to occur increasingly outside the framework of history, assume forms which resemble geological processes. The rules which "historic man" has formulated in the course of millennia no longer apply. (Z, 6, 575)

Jünger then turns from scientific to philosophical speculations, from geology to what might be called "geosophy," or a metaphysics of the earth. He sets out to explore, to fathom the "Erdsinn der menschlichen Tätigkeit" (Z, 6, 573), the meaning of human activity as it relates to the earth. On the face of it, this phrase is ambiguous. It could be understood narrowly, in the manner of the historian, of, say, Hegel, who was solely concerned with man, and who "spiritualized" the course of human events. Jünger rejects such concepts as being restrictive because they exclude the consideration of man as he relates to nature and the earth. He rather believes "dass das Sein im Urgrund und nicht im Geist wohnt" (Z, 6, 574), that the quintessence of things does not dwell in the "universal spirit" but in the earth. (In the context of this quotation, "Urgrund" means "matrix of all things," not "primal cause.")

One may assume that the "Urgrund" strives toward spiritualization ["Vergeistigung"] in which endeavor it also uses man as an instrument. This would constitute a new beginning of the spiritualization of the earth, of which there have been many. Man's role and responsibility would be to help this process along and prevent it from crystallizing magically.

Or one may favor the theory that man — ever more clearly realizing what he is involved in — penetrates a number of strata, the last of which was called "history," to reach the "Urgrund" and spiritualize parts of it. Wherever he comes in contact with it, the result will be powerful answers. (Z, 6, 573)

This statement, representative as it is of Jünger's metaphysical speculations, poses difficulties that beggar the interpretative imagination. It poses questions that resist an answer. What is meant by the numerous instances of the earth's "spiritualization" that have occurred in the past? What is "magic crystallization"? What could those "powerful answers" be which are the response of man's contact with the "Urgrund"? Once again, we must turn to the myth to be enlightened. For Jünger, there are chthonic as well as divine forces; the earth as well as the heavens is endowed with great powers which, from time to time, engage in momentous cosmic struggles. Gaia, the goddess of the earth, was the wife of Uranos, who personified the sky and was also thought to be the supreme god. She instigated the Titan Cronos, their son, to rise against Uranos. He did so, prevailed over him and emasculated him. On another occasion, Gaia induced all the Titans to do battle with the Olympian gods. Hercules, a demigod, also engaged in a similar encounter. And now, man is involved in a similar upheaval of the earth asserting itself. This upheaval is preceded by the overthrow of the gods, the momentous event of these last centuries, of the final phase of "history." Religion increasingly loses its power over man, a process which may be termed the "secularization of the Western mind." This is the true meaning of Nietzsche's oft-quoted dictum "God is dead," as well as of Léon Bloy's conviction that "Dieu se retire." The earth has become godless ground; as a result, enormous energies have been released. Man is hard at work, laboring frantically yet without direction, without knowing what he is doing. This is chaos, but a new order will be established. Man not only unfetters but will also effectively and creatively control the chthonic forces. It is the earth, which Jünger believes to be an entity endowed with will and exhibiting intent, that imposes this task on man, its ingenious and willing son.

It is the "Arbeiter" who is most conscious of the task at hand and who is unquestioningly ready to perform it. Jünger finds it significant that current theories describe the origin of the universe as a violent event (the "big bang"). He comments: "The cosmogonic conceptions of our time involve designs of dynamic global models. Although the scope is enormous, they can be measured in terms of both time and space. Precise information is already available. Its basic elements, dynamics and exactitude, correspond to the very nature of the 'Arbeiter.' Explosion plays a role in matters both large and small, as well as in regard to both origin and end" (Z, 6, 533).

Exploration of the cosmos is eminently the domain of the "Arbeiter." Although man had not yet ventured into space at the time when Jünger was writing *An der Zeitmauer,* he confidently states: "Space travel provides the evidence that the "Arbeiter" has attained to lordly rank. It is among his pleasures, similar to the nobleman's indulging in the hunt, the king's manner of making war [!] or involving himself in architecture" (Z, 6, 546,).

An der Zeitmauer is a sequel to *Der Arbeiter,* rather than its second part. The author has now fully fashioned the cosmic framework of his ideas, has developed his philosophical premises and looked farther into the future. In the first essay, he was preoccupied with the issues of the day — as he saw them — engaging in polemics. The center of gravity was politics; in the *Zeitmauer,* it is metaphysics. When Jünger wrote *Der Arbeiter,* he was an activist. Twenty-five years later, he had long since withdrawn from politics. His stance was now that of the detached observer indulging cosmic visions and visions of man to be.

CHAPTER 11

The Psychonaut

O NE of Jünger's most recent books, published at the age of seventy-five, is a remarkable undertaking. It deals with drugs and drug-taking; it is entitled *Annäherungen: Drogen und Rausch* (1970). "Annäherung" means "approach" as well as "approximation": approach to the absolute, quintessential reality as well as approximation of insight into this reality. "Rausch" also carries two meanings; it connotes both "intoxication" and "ecstasy." "Rausch" is a state engendered by a strong stimulative such as alcohol or a drug; but it may also be induced by ascetic abstinence.

Annäherungen is by no means intended to appeal to or, indeed, exploit the recent fashion. Jünger is an old hand at experimenting with drugs. Between 1918 and 1922 he used ether, cocaine, opium, and hashish. After a lapse of thirty years, it was the hallucinogenic effects of mescaline, ololuiqui (the Mexican mushroom), and lysergic acid diethalamide (LSD) that commanded his interest. The dates are important: the impending debacle of World War I, the chaos that followed, and the years after the fateful, thoroughly unsettling second global conflict impelled Jünger to seek new insights and new certainties. Moreover, his use of drugs is cyclopedic; in this regard it is without parallel. But his approach has always been that of the experimentalist, the man of the "adventurous heart." He has never taken drugs habitually and, unlike De Quincey or Baudelaire, has never been an addict.

Annäherungen is a log book, the account of the author's voyages on the uncharted seas of the soul. This record is broadened by references to both literary and scientific sources. Men like De Quincey *(Confessions of an English Opium-Eater),* Baudelaire *(Les Paradis artificiels),* and Aldous Huxley *(The Doors of Perception)* are cited for comparison and contrast, but also for widening the horizon. The scientific literature has been consulted. Jünger has known, and shared his experiments with, Rudolf Gelpke, author of the provocative *Vom Rausch im Orient und Okzident* (1966), and Albert Hofmann, who synthetically produced the alkaloid LSD. And since experiments and readings are often recorded within a rich context of circumstances, *Annäherungen* incorporates a good many autobiographical excursuses. It all adds up to a five-hundred-page essay. And, ultimately, *Annäherungen* is a septuagenarian's testimonial embodying the wisdom filtered from the press of old age.

The motivation that has led Jünger to take drugs is threefold. He has found them to enhance his vitality, and to enliven his adventurousness, his seeking of risk and hazard. Drugs also afforded him stimulation in his irrepressible quest for metaphysical insight. He wanted to find the New World, not in the manner of the Genoese who matched "the vast and furious ocean," but as a Columbus "on a higher plane." Jünger was motivated, indeed driven, by what Baudelaire called "le goût de l'infini." Finally, Jünger used drugs as "the catapult fronting the wall of time, the wall separating the present era," which he believes is drawing to a close, from the new eon. He hoped, by dint of the drug, to vault this wall or, at least, to appreciate more fully "the great transition" ("der Grosse Übergang") because he is convinced that drugs liberate from what he considers rapidly outmoded ways of thinking and perceiving. It is the propellant power of the drug that might enable him to rise above, and perhaps also to break through, "the wall of time."

Jünger knows full well that taking drugs may be fatal; he was sure of that beyond the cavil of a doubt when an overdose of hashish almost killed him. But this did not deter him — on the contrary. He had sought that "narrow strip separating life from death" on the battlefield, and the sea had shown its lethal powers in his encounter with a stinging ray and in a narrow escape from drowning. Life enthralls, and death fascinates, him. In the fashion of the mystic, he seeks the oneness of all being, a state in which life and death are no longer antithetical or irreconcilable. This mystic union or, rather, unity is never fully accomplished this side of existence, but "Annäherung" is possible. Drugs serve this end; hence their lure.

Since a full treatment of *Annäherungen* is, within the framework of this study, impossible, my exposition will be limited to Jünger's experimentation with drugs. Extensive quotations will be used to indicate the yield of the several experiments and, equally characteristic, the experimentalist's descriptive manner.

In the fall of 1918, while recovering from a wound sustained in action, Jünger made his first voyage to the *terra incognita* of the soul. What led him to undertake it was curiosity, the boredom of a slow recovery, or even a sense of sauciness or recklessness. He had used ether before, but only as the entomologist does. He also knew about the use of ether as a drug. He had read Maupassant's short story "Rêves," had even translated it. (The manuscript is lost.)

After inhaling ether, Jünger traversed three stages: intoxication (Rausch) — narcotic numbness (or stupor) — lucid exhilaration:

Numbness (or stupor) had been followed by a phase of lucid exhilaration. Intoxication had led into a deep well — in a manner that was reminiscent of, but not identical with, Maupassant's description. [It was an experience of the ear.] I *heard* it all — like the bright opening motive of an orchestra, which a second one took up, modulating and transmuting it. The echo was taken up in the manner of a reflection, becoming deeper in the process. After a brief pause, the first orchestra set in again. Both were very distant from one another but gradually moved closer while some of the instruments ceased playing. Just prior to the narcotic stage, image and reflection became one, were fused, the music changing to a roar of marked wavelength. I heard what I had seen: a web or woof. Then the sound drew back into the strings, which no longer vibrated. It tired, becoming too deep to be heard. (Ann, 220)

Ether had sharpened the senses but also demonstrated that they are as one sense: what is heard can also be seen. The experience was synesthetic, it pointed to the union, the oneness of which the mystics speak.

Maupassant set down his experience thus:

. . . I took a large flask of ether and, lying down, began, slowly, to inhale.

After a few minutes I thought I heard a vague murmur, which soon changed to a kind of humming, and it seemed to me that the inside of my body was getting as light as vaporizing air. Some sort of torpor followed, a somnolent well-being in spite of persistent pains. [The protagonist suffered from violent neuralgia.] But they ceased to be excruciating: it was now the kind of suffering that one accepts since it was no longer that frightful feeling of being torn apart against which the body protests.

Soon the strange and pleasant feeling of vacuity in my breast began to spread, extending to my limbs, making them light as if flesh and bones had melted away. Only the skin remained, which was necessary to let me feel the sweetness of living, of being enveloped in well-being. Then I became aware that I was suffering no more. The pain was gone, had melted away, had evaporated. And I heard voices, four voices, two dialogues, without understanding what was said. Now they were but indistinct sounds, now I understood single words. But I realized it was a kind of humming, registered by my ears. I was not sleeping; I was awake. I understood, felt, reasoned so keenly, so profoundly, with such extraordinary power that a joy of mind came over me, a strange intoxication, brought about by the uncoupling of my mental faculties.

This was not a dream induced by hashish; these were not the somewhat morbid visions produced by it — this was very keen reasoning, a new way of seeing, of judging, of appreciating the things of life, and with a certainty and the absolute awareness that this way was the true one.

And then the ancient image of the Holy Writ suddenly arose in my mind. It seemed to me that I had eaten from the Tree of Knowledge, that all mysteries were being revealed to me — so powerful was the dominion of the new, strange, irrefutable logic. I was thronged by arguments, reasons, proofs that were immediately reversed by stronger proofs, reasons and arguments. My head had been turned into a battlefield of ideas. I was a superior being, armed with invincible intelligence. The pleasure, as I realized my power, was prodigious.

This lasted a long, long time. I kept inhaling from the flask. Suddenly I noticed that it was empty. The chagrin I felt was frightening. ("Rêves," 1881)

During the same period, Jünger tried opium, drinking a brown, bitter tincture. As he was falling asleep, he felt as if he were changing vehicles or, rather, shifting into high gear. And, again, there was this ambivalence: time moved more slowly and, at the same time, more rapidly. It was like riding in an airplane; one knows that one moves fast, yet, looking out of the window, it seems as if one were merely creeping along.

Awake again, he went for a drink of water:

Hearing the glass fill up — it was as if I were ascending stairs while being aware of very delicate temporal cadences and spatial structures. At such moments, anything can be an instrument, though these differ — like the hours. Each has its own resonance. The midnight melody sounds different at two o'clock. . . .

Still standing in the bathroom, hearing the glass fill up, hearing the harmony created by the mobile playing upon the immobile. Both were translucent — the running water and the quartz crystal. In the sucking manner of a polyp, the ear attached to the round shape of the glass, moving upward as the water level rose. Then it glided into the whirling water. It was *I* that was playing its song. Or rather: it was not I ensconced in the innermost core of matter but hand, glass, and water had entered *my* innermost being as if it were a magic chamber. No matter: my brother's [Friedrich Georg Jünger] verse applied, in every way:

. . . melody and instrument are one.

When harmony and melody meet, time is immaterial. Delight does not endure, else art would cease to be. (Ann, 283, 284)

The images that the draft of opium conjured up remained strangely abstract. There are the "correspondences" of solid and liquid matter, of temporal cadences and spatial structures, of mobile and immobile substances — leading to a sense of identity, the oneness of instrument and the melody produced, also of harmony and melody.

The yield is meagre compared, for instance, to the vast array of visions and images, joys and pains recorded by De Quincey, who had also seen "water":

. . . dreams of lakes and silvery expanses of water.
. . . The waters gradually changed their character — from translucent lakes, shining like mirrors, they became seas and oceans. And now a tremendous change. . . . Hitherto the human face had often mixed in my dreams, but not despotically, nor with any special power of tormenting. But now that affection which I have called the tyranny of the human face began to unfold itself.
. . now it was that upon the rocking waters of the ocean the human face began to reveal itself; the sea appeared paved with innumerable faces, upturned to the heavens; faces, imploring, wrathful, despairing; faces surged upward by the thousands, by myriads, by generations: infinite was my agitation; my mind tossed, as it seemed, upon the billowy oceans, and weltered upon the weltering waves. *(Confessions of an Opium-Eater,* Part III: "The Pains of Opium")

Jünger records abstractions of limited scope. By contrast, the Englishman portrays visions of cosmic range yielding both pleasure and pain. Although Jünger himself points to these differences, he had experimented with opium but once, while De Quincey had used the drug habitually, for more than fifteen years, when he set down his confessions.

The hemp plant yields hallucinogenic potency in two forms. Jünger did not smoke marijuana but rather ingested that extract of hemp which is called hashish. Having done so, he turned to reading in the *Arabian Nights,* appropriately so, because some of its stories doubtless relate hashish-induced dreams of visions. The drug took effect:

The images were powerful and immediate; they were unreflected. Heretofore they had been shining like light in the mirror — now I saw light itself, very close by. I had read the text; now I heard the original version. This was not reading any more. The story revealed a depth I had never thought possible. It afforded access to the sea and its monotony. He who heard it was penetrated by it, needed the text no more, needed the letters no more. I put the book down. I breathed faster and more pleasurably. Breathing was, in every instance, a delight I was conscious of. It was as if my diaphragm were being lightly touched. The touches were rhythmic, a pendulum gently stroking me. It described a wide arc, came back, touching me again, a little more strongly, more tenderly. . . . It rose and swung back, its momentum increasing. Now I traveled with it, upwards. . . . I had entered into the pendulum's weight: into the gondola of a large swing. Its keel, though sharply cut, barely touched my skin. It was the draft of air that stroked it. My sensitivity increased as the swing rose again. High up, I felt giddy and burst out laughing. Then the whistling descent began. The motion was not to be stopped, nor to be controlled. The speed was such that a plunge seemed imminent. Deep pleasure had followed upon hilarity. Now there was doubt, then fear — in rapid succession. . . . The feeling of discomfort did not set in gradually; it hit me full strength. The gondola traveled with undiminished speed but as if the gears had been shifted to reverse.

I jumped up and, looking in the mirror, no longer knew myself. There — a pale face distorted by laughter. It was stronger than mine, showing hostile disposition. He — that man opposite me — was planning to harm me. I must not let go of him.

The dose I had taken must have been much too strong. It could be lethal. (Ann, 314)

The first part of this passage describes a change that is both sudden and radical: from rationally conscious insight yielding but limited understanding to a full, unencumbered one, from seeing the text to hearing "the original version." "Original version": this may also mean the story as the narrator had envisioned it but could not tell to his satisfaction — every work of art falls short of what the artist imagines and intends.

Then the pendulum swings into view. Touching ever so lightly, it yields a feeling of exquisite tenderness which, paradoxically, is enhanced as the pendulum strokes more strongly. Finally, subject and object are disparate entities no longer. The dreamer has entered into the weight of the pendulum, partakes of it and its action. Yet there is consciousness of pleasure, of hilarity. Then doubt sets in; fear seizes him as he confronts the image in the mirror. It is he, but also his fearsome enemy intent upon doing him harm.

It turned out that Jünger had indeed taken too large a dose of hashish (or perhaps, the years had increased its potency). The dose might have been lethal, had not a physician, quickly summoned, ministered to the victim.

Thirty years went by. Jünger had traversed the Occident (ether, cocaine) and the Orient (opium, hashish); now he was ready to embark on the third stage of his voyage — to Mexico (mescaline, psilocybin, LSD). Jünger justifies the inclusion of the latter in this grouping by pointing to the close relationship (regarding substance as well as effect) between lysergic acid diethalamide and lysergic acid amide, which the Mexican drug ololuiqui contains. Mexico is therefore understood as a "mental" rather than a geographical concept.

Jünger describes how he was affected by chewing the Mexican hallucinogenic mushroom teonacatl, which contains psilocybin:

Everything was skin, and it was being touched, the retina too. Touch turned to light. This light was multicolored; it formed strings, gently swaying to and fro like the glass bead strings of an Oriental curtain. They formed the kind of door through which one enters in his dreams — curtains of lust and danger. Wind moved them like a raiment, like the string skirts of a dancer, opening and closing to the swaying of the hips. The beads gave forth murmuring sounds, playing on the sharpened senses. By contrast, the jingling of the silver bracelets and anklets was too loud. A smell obtained, of sweat, blood, tobacco, chopped horse hair, cheap attar of roses. They must be carrying on in the stables, but who knows?

It must be a huge palace, of the Mauritanian kind, a disreputable place no doubt. Rooms adjoined the dance halls, whole suites extending to the basement. And curtains everywhere, glittering, sparkling radioactively. Also this murmuring of glass instruments, coquettishly enticing. . . . Now it ceased, now it started up again, more importunately, more insistently — almost certain of my yielding. Then things became distinct: historical collages, *vox humana,* call of the cuckoo. Was it the Whore of Santa Lucia thrusting out her breasts at the window? . . . Salome dancing, her amber necklace emitting sparks, her nipples rising to firmness. What doesn't one do for his John? Damn this obscenity! But it wasn't I who said this; it had been whispered through the curtain.

The snakes were filthy, lazily lolling on the floor mats, barely alive. They were studded with diamond slivers. Some, eyes red and green, peered from the ceiling. And all this glitter, this whispering, hissing, blinking. . . . Silence, and then it came again, softer but more importunate. They had got me. . . .

The madam came in through the curtain, a busy woman, passing me obliviously. I saw her red-heeled boots. The garters cut deep into the fleshy thighs. Huge breasts, the delta of the Amazon; parrots, piranhas, semiprecious stones everywhere.

Then she went into the kitchen — or were there cellars, too? The glitter, the whispering, the hissing and blinking became indistinguishable but also more concentrated and, finally, expectant, jubilant.

It became hot, unbearably so. I got up . . . (Ann, 466)

Jünger's sensitivity had been heightened *and* widened. All his skin, even the surface of the eye, was touched. Then the ambivalence of sensory perception manifested itself. What he felt, he also saw: light of many colors assuming shapes in motion. This was the matrix — the matrix of image and vision.

Then light became matter, turning to bead strings the kind of which Oriental curtains and the skirts of dancers are made. What is seen is also heard: the swishing of these strings. So greatly sharpened was the sense of hearing that the jingling of bracelet and anklet almost hurt the ear. Then the sense of smell came into play: disconcerting, warning odors, wafting in from the stables, seemingly the place of dubious, dangerous goings-on. Had he not entered through "curtains of lust and danger"?

He finds himself inside a palace. However, it strikes him as a questionable kind of place. Nobody about: his unease grows as the curtains glow dangerously; glass instruments murmur alluringly, temptingly.

As things become distinct to eye and ear, it is clear that this is indeed a realm of "lust and danger." The Whore of Santa Lucia (who is she?) exhibits her massive charms; Salome dances, unmistakable in her intent. The snakes, eminently creatures of the earth, are here creatures of filth; agility has turned into inertness. But they also lurk from above, with eyes that fascinate and frighten.

This is the far-flung realm of lustful pleasures. The cleavage of the madam's bosom widens to a delta — the delta of that vast river traversing the torrid region. There are parrots, birds of the most splendid plumage, and piranhas, most vicious and aggressive.

The awakening is sudden, the heat having become unendurable. The drug-eater knows both pleasure and pain.

Jünger also took mescaline, the hallucinogenic drug extracted from mescal (or peyote), a cactus indigenous to Mexico and the southwestern United States. The experiment was not only recorded but also yielded — by dint of fictional elaboration — the central passage of the story *Besuch auf Godenholm* (Visit on Godenholm) [1950]. The notes on the experiment will be related to comparable passages from *The Doors of Perception* (1954), Aldous Huxley's comprehensive study of mescaline.

Jünger: Sitting at the window, I looked out upon an expanse of snow. Every painter knows that snow is of many colors but here it brought forth — in ever-increasing emanations — clouds and waves of luminescent matter. A flame shot up; the sparks — scintillulae — which were woven into it, broke away. (Ann, 487)

Huxley: . . . How significant is the enormous heightening, under mescaline, of the perception of color. . . . Mescaline raises all colors to a higher power and makes the percipient aware of innumerable fine shades of differences, to which, at ordinary times, he is completely blind. . . . Like mescaline takers, many mystics perceive supernaturally brilliant colors, not only with the outward eye, but even in the objective world around them. *(The Doors of Perception)*

Huxley's corroboration is significant, but more so is his insistence on the similarity of the drug-induced and the traditional mystic vision. Jünger, on the other hand, exhibits in subsequent passages a sharpened sensibility in his appreciation of painting, particularly that of the twentieth century. (It is an odd fact that Jünger, being an *Augenmensch* rather than an *Ohrenmensch,* only rarely refers to the visual arts in his writings.)

Upon a mystic insight, there follows a most tangible vision of the powers inherent in books and of the nature of authorship:

Jünger: I was also aware of distance. I heard a dog barking: it was the Fenris Wolf [a powerful demonic beast, according to Nordic mythology]. The froth on his maw became the Milky Way. But here space was not without life. There was animated tension, something like expectation. I was somehow in accord but it was weird. I went to and fro, then sat down in an armchair and looked at the books. Their spines rose, forming veritable towers. I had not known the power inherent in them. Print, title pages, text were inconsequential, mere reflections, Platonic shadings of mental power. Authorship is a miniscule loan. (Ann, 487)

Huxley: Like flowers, they [the books] glowed when I looked at them with brighter colors, a profounder significance. Red books, like rubies; emerald books, books bound in white jade;\books of agate; of aquamarine, of yellow topaz, lapis lazuli, books whose color was so intense, so intrinsically meaningful, that they seemed on the point of leaving the shelves to thrust themselves more insistently on my attention. *(Doors of Perception)*

Jünger's vision then abruptly changed to archetype and totem animal:

It would not do to see the phenomena, even the mere phenomena, always like this. It is a good thing that perception filters them, that the senses separate them, that the word fixes them. I went over to where my son was sitting at the table. The meal was over. My wife came in through the door, hands folded over her breast. She bore herself like a priestess. Ample sleeves, touching the floor. And then she stood there, bright against the door frame. I saw her in the capacity of her office and mission, saw also my son's totem animal.

The end of the passage seeks to describe that the (non-religious) *unio mystica* was achieved:

I was all right. I sat a long time, contemplating them [wife and son] in the quiet peaceful room. As fire from snow, so, now, power and confidence were instilled in me. When I later thought about all this, it struck me that no word was spoken. Distances never to be traversed threaten to separate us from what quintessentially is if we fail in our attempt at *Annäherung*. But if we succeed, everything is bound together, coalesces. Outside and inside, past and future begin to fuse. The world is felt to be a home. (Ann, 488)

When Jünger began taking drugs, he was one of a few. Now it is a fashion, but he believes that drugs will play an enduring as well as an expanding role in our culture.

CHAPTER 12

Die Zwille

IN *Annäherungen,* Jünger had turned to recounting his experimentation, the ways in which various drugs play on the mind. Once again he relived the past. In a novel, he subsequently reminisced about his boyhood, about a time antedating his African escapade; it is entitled *Die Zwille* (The Slingshot [1973]). The title significantly refers to an instrument appropriate to *homo ludens,* a plaything which may also be put to dangerous, even fatal use.

The action takes place in the early years of the century when, with interruptions, the author attended the Gymnasium in Hannover and Braunschweig. Although, or just because, he was intelligent and imaginative, school bored him. The result was nothing short of disaster. The report for the year which the novel describes lists only "5's" (F's), the exception being music ("Singen") in which he received a D ("4"). The report card also noted: "Promotion to the next higher grade utterly impossible." (But Jünger eventually managed to complete his secondary education. When he graduated, the war had broken out and, luckily, the requirements for the "Abitur" had been lowered for those enlisting in the armed forces.) Since his parents had moved to the country, he attended school in the city, while, together with a number of fellow students, living with one of the teachers.

Although Jünger describes his boyhood days, *Die Zwille* is not an autobiographical novel; it is therefore, dissimilar to *Afrikanische Spiele* because the protagonist is not the author himself. This role is played by two pupils: a boy of ten named Clamor, that is, a lonely soul "crying out in pain and fear," and Teo, a *Primaner,* seven or eight years his senior. Yet the author has endowed them with certain of his own traits and propensities.

Die Zwille is a psychological novel about pupils and teachers and their mutual relationship. It also affords good insight into the secondary education and, by extension, the life in village and city during the Wilhelminian era — an era of security and peace which, however, was rapidly drawing to a close. And by centering the story on two boys, the author gave himself the opportunity of dealing extensively with the element of play, the child being both the ingenuous and versatile embodiment of *homo ludens*.

The novel is divided into three parts. Part One, "Wie kam er hierher?" (How did he get here?), describes how Clamor left the village of Oldhorst to attend the Gymnasium in Braunschweig while living at Professor Quarisch's boardinghouse. The boy's antecedents are fully explored as well as those of Teo, who comes from the same village. In Part Two ("Die Pension") both boys now live in the boardinghouse. This part deals with its regimen and the boys' life in school and after hours. The concluding chapter is labelled "Zielübungen" (Target Practice). The slingshot, a specimen equally magnificent and expensive, has finally been acquired. It is being tested, but an untoward event precludes its crowning use, leading to the dramatic end of Clamor's brief academic career.

Clamor Ebling's antecedents are lowly, his early years unhappy. Bereft of his mother, his sole source of love and certainty is his father who, a miller's helper, dies from overexertion. Herr Braun, his employer, assumes the orphan's guardianship and renders a secondary education possible. School is not easy for Clamor, his mind being that of an artist rather than of a scholar. He is lonely but also uncertain of himself, defenseless and therefore constantly beset by fear. "Everywhere he was threatened by traps, snares, the hammer hitting him from above" (Zw, 50). Although he has no reason to dread it, he is certain he will be expelled from school, a wholly baseless fear. But the "hammer" falls. Clamor, the guileless fool, is victimized, not by his doing but by circumstance.

Although yearning to belong, he has neither companion nor friend. His life, his scant pleasures are of the solitary kind. On lonely walks he indulges his imagination, collects pebbles, pieces of glass and crockery, an occasional bead and button: little worthless things which, however, satisfy his delicate sense of form and color.

It is a world of fantasy in which he finds temporary solace, even satisfaction. Sometimes he thinks

he might be involved in a game whose significance was concealed from him. He was perhaps the son of a mighty king and had been sent into this city as a scout. But why? — he had only the vaguest of notions. Why didn't he *know* it? Yes, he thought to himself, without this fear, the game would probably not be real. Yet the sense of estrangement remained. What is my obligation here? What have I done? How did I get here? (Zw, 60)

The minister of Oldhorst, Professor Quarisch's brother, takes an interest in Clamor, preparing him for the Gymnasium. In a sense, they are kindred souls, both beset, even tormented, by a sense of failure. Although he gains outward recognition — the minister is promoted to the position of "Superintendant" (administrator of a church district), a fact which earns him the nickname "Superus" — he is painfully aware of being but a poor preacher. Owing to his weakness, he loses both Sybille, his wife, and Teo, his son. Vicar Simmerlin, personable and strong but ruthless, has won Sybille's love and Teo's affection. He induces them to go away with him, to live an adventurous life in the Near East. A domestic drama in an improbable setting: a village parsonage. But although the catastrophe is some time in coming, Superus has not the strength to prevent it. As *dramatis persona* he is but a pathetic figure, and he knows it: "The drama is castrated — a play for a doll's house" (Zw, 82). Superus suffers a blow from which he never recovers: the loss of self-respect. And so he imagines the macabre inscription on his tombstone to be: "Here lies the failure of Oldhorst, failure as husband, father, minister" (Zw, 71).

He has become estranged from his wife; she turns away from him. Teo even turns against him, becomes his enemy. Superus calls him "Absalom," the son who rose against his father. More tellingly, he also speaks of him as "the marten that gnaws at my heart" (Zw, 72) because he cannot but pity himself. Unaware or not, he knows that the German word for marten is "Marder." Changing one letter, the word becomes "Mörder," that is, murderer. Teo viciously reciprocates, by calling him "die Quappe" (tadpole), a small creature without bone or spine. (It may be noted that the author's deep interest in the animal is also reflected in the way he portrays these two characters.)

Teo is the very antithesis of his father: strong, coldly intelligent and unscrupulous. He is a "Herr" (Zw, 53), master or lord in the way he thinks and acts. To him life is play, a game in which he tests and asserts his strength and skill. Uncertainty and danger is the atmosphere in which he thrives. He likes to play with dangerous things: weapons (particularly guns), dynamite, poison. His instincts are those of the hunter; people are his game — in both senses of the word. Thus the story centers on a plaything which may be put to dangerous and, indeed, nefarious use: a slingshot — not an ordinary one, but the best and most expensive of its kind. Employing most unscrupulous means, he acquires it; made to serve a manhunt, it victimizes — unintentionally and by chance — Clamor. In Teo's eyes, it is a deplorable but certainly reparable accident.

It is clear that Teo is antithetical not only to his father but also to his young companion: "Teo was as strong as he, Clamor, was weak" (Zw, 238); "Teo played dangerous games, but Clamor dreamed" (Zw, 324).

The second part of the novel ("Die Pension") describes not only life at the boardinghouse but also the school which Clamor and Teo attend. The latter is a Gymnasium typical of the time before World War I. The almost exclusively academic curriculum is designed to prepare the student for a professional career. Discipline is stern and rigidly enforced; corporal punishment is meted out even for minor transgressions. Students and teachers are not bound by trust and respect but consider each other adversaries. Though pervasive, the spirit of rebelliousness rarely leads to overt action against the authority.

The principal presides over, indeed rules, the hierarchically ordered faculty. The teachers do not conceal their sense of superiority regarding their colleagues who teach "nonacademic" subjects, such as art and physical education. The students call them "Proleten" (plebeians), unwittingly sharing this dubious sense of superiority; but they also recognize the foibles and weaknesses of the "Kathederhelden" (heroes of the rostrum). A hierarchical order also governs the students. The young among them defer to the older boys and are happy when they gain their condescending companionship.

This is the ambience into which Clamor is suddenly cast. In Oldhorst he was lonely and forlorn after his father had died although, in some measure he was sustained by his benevolent guardian and Superus, who was helpful and fond of him. Among his contemporaries, he had no friends. But all this was as nothing compared to what he now has to contend with: the country boy has to adjust to life in a bustling city, has to be equal to the competitive demands of the Gymnasium, has to harden himself against a multitude of people who consider lowly antecedents a blemish and sensitivity a sign of weakness. Fear has dominated his life; now it fairly overpowers him.

School is an ordeal. Already on his lonely walk to the forbidding fortress of learning (the other boys ride bicycles), his encounters strike him as strange and hostile, filling his timid mind with in-creasing fear. He passes a drill ground where the sergeant, martinet incarnate, puts the recruits through frightening paces. Inmates of the nearby jail, browbeaten, pathetic, are marched by him, on their way to work. Even the workers of the textile factory strike him as strange: their appearance, their conduct, their crude banter.

The day in school begins with chapel, welcome, soothing moments of respite. But the first (and worst) hour is fast in coming: mathematics. Dr. Hilpert conducts the course, condescendingly, in-sensitively. He thinks that he is wasting his time on immature, un-receptive minds. He is an embittered man because a university posi-tion has been denied him. Embodying the narrow analytical mind, he senses at once that he and Clamor, who is imaginative and creatively endowed, differ radically. Insecure as he really is, Dr. Hilpert sees in this little timid boy a challenge to what he is and stands for. So he takes it out on him, an easy but cruel action because Clamor, aca-demically ungifted, is a poor mathematician.

The only subject in which the boy excels is art. Herr Mühlbauer, his teacher, is, at least in his own eyes, a "failure" because he is a painter manqué. However, in contrast to his colleague, he does not visit his disappointment on the pupils. He understands Clamor, likes and helps him, affording him rare hours of certainty and fulfillment. When the boy's hour of failure comes, he stands by him.

Life at the boardinghouse is also dark, and the moments of light are equally rare.

Professor Quarisch, a teacher at the Gymnasium, presides over the "Pension." Academically competent, he also teaches well because he understands and likes his students. Strong, certain of himself, he dis-penses the proper blend of discipline and freedom to his charges. (Another instance of antithetical characters: he and his brother, the Superus, are worlds apart.) The Professor is ably assisted by his wife Mally; together they have established and smoothly enforce the daily routine, which is described in full detail: the living arrangements, matutinal hygiene, the common meals, etc.

The quarters are spacious. It is an old house, the rambling sort, with all kinds of nearly inaccessible additions. The "Alkoven," located in a remote part, is occupied by Teo, Clamor, and Buz, the latter a "gerissener Dummkopf" (smart blockhead) who is not at all concerned about his inevitable academic failure. His interest is horses and the military; he wants to be a cavalry man. These boys have only one thing in common: they all come from Oldhorst. Having found surreptitious access to a disused room, they withdraw to the "Kabinett" to discuss their schemes, the ways of making full and exciting use of their scant leisure time.

Teo, by virtue of age, intelligence, and his domineering personality, plans and directs the conspiratorial ventures. Clamor and Buz are his "Leibwächter" (bodyguards), wholly subservient, mere pawns in questionable and dangerous games. The objects of Teo's kind of "play" are people; his aim is to indulge his prowess and cunning, to gain dominance over others. He knows no scruples. "Understand the laws but don't be bound by them" (Zw, 165) is his maxim.

The "master" plays at being detective: tracking down dubious characters: Dranthé, a respectable businessman but ill-camouflaged homophile; Zaddeck, vice principal at the Gymnasium, a sadistic deviate who physically abuses his charges; and the "Penner" (hoboes) who, beyond the pale of the law, carry on in "Ungers Garten," an unused park.

The hoboes are to be the object of the "crowning" venture; the attempt to prevail over them by frightening and dispersing them. But how could three boys gain the upper hand over grown-ups? By the clever use of the "Zwille," the slingshot, by using the plaything as a weapon. It can be used as such most efficaciously because it is silent and leaves no traces. The range is not inconsiderable, and the marksman employing concealment remains undetected.

Obtaining such an implement is difficult because Teo, "der Herr," will not settle for less than the best of its kind; but the price, ten marks, is beyond his meager means. To get hold of the slingshot, he resorts to dubious methods. Extorting the money from a rich boy fails. But then he finds — and keeps — the golden ten-mark piece which Buz, when he was sent shopping by Frau Mally, had lost. Wholly subservient to Teo, Buz only mildly objects and accepts the punishment for his carelessness. When Teo plays his games, he refuses to be bound by moral considerations.

Games such as Teo has planned require careful preparation. The victims must be known thoroughly, their habits and, particularly, their weaknesses. They are therefore "shadowed," a task which is assigned to the two "bodyguards." Clamor is uneasy about this sort of thing but submits because he, like Buz, is completely dominated by the older boy.

The third and concluding part of the novel is entitled "Zielübungen" (Target Practice). Teo now owns the coveted implement; Buz and Clamor are equipped with the lowly, homemade kind — with "Bauernzwillen" (peasant slingshots), as Teo derogatorily calls them. They are being tried out first on stationary targets such as bottles and cans, then, by Buz, on toads and rats while Teo, characteristically, chooses as his target a woodpecker, a bird of resplendent plumage. Clamor is drawn into all this, especially the killing of animals, against his inclination and will. He proves himself an inept marksman, hurting his thumb rather than hitting the target. But then: why does he allow himself to be involved in these distateful games? Teo brooks neither reluctance nor disobedience, and, equally important, Clamor is a lonely and frightened boy who desperately needs companionship, needs to "belong," whatever the price.

Having developed a good measure of skill, they now seek out a more demanding and dangerous target. Vice Principal Zaddeck, the sex deviate, has been shadowed; his lodgings are clearly identified — or presumably so. Shooting at his windows, they want to thoroughly frighten, perhaps even "break," the man who lives in constant danger of being found out. The "Bauernzwille" causes no damage, only noise and nervous investigation on the part of the presumed Herr Zaddeck. The next evening, Teo, employing his more powerful implement, shatters a window. He and Buz rapidly flee, but Clamor, timid and uncertain, is nabbed by — Major von Olten's orderly, Buz having failed to properly identify the target.

The major reports the incident to the principal, and Clamor is expelled. The fear of his dreams has come true. It never occurs to him — such is his unquestioning sense of loyalty — to implicate the actual perpetrator. The latter accepts this fateful silence because he is certain, but wrongly so, that he can extricate Clamor from his predicament. "For Teo, this was nothing but play; he, Clamor, paid for it with his skin" (Zw, 289).

Yet the novel ends on a conciliatory note, almost in the dubious manner of a happy ending. Herr Mühlbauer, the art teacher, to whom Clamor was devoted, but whom, on a previous occasion, he had unintentionally but grievously offended — pathetic fellow that he was — comes to the rescue of the distraught boy, inviting him to live at his house, affording him parental love and understanding preceptorship.

With *Die Zwille*, the septuagenarian author has added a further dimension to his work: a social and essentially psychological novel. It also offers a variation on the enduring theme of *homo ludens*.

Selected Bibliography

PRIMARY SOURCES

1. Books

The list comprises Ernst Jünger's writings as they originally appeared in book form. For complete biographical details, see Hans Peter Des Coudres, *Bibliographie der Werke Ernst Jüngers* (Stuttgart: Klett, 1970). This exhaustive work also registers all editions, most of which have been revised more than once and often thoroughly. The sole exception is *Der Arbeiter*.

In Stahlgewittern: Aus dem Tagebuch eines Stosstruppführers v. Ernst Jünger, Kriegsfreiwilliger, dann Leutnant und Kompanieführer im Füs.-Regt. Prinz Albrecht von Preussen (Hannov. Nr. 73). Hannover: privately printed, 1920.

Der Kampf als inneres Erlebnis. Berlin: Mittler, 1922.

Das Wäldchen 125: Eine Chronik aus den Grabenkämpfen 1918. Berlin: Mittler, 1925.

Feuer und Blut: Ein kleiner Ausschnitt aus einer grossen Schlacht. Magedeburg: Stahlhelm-Verlag, 1925.

Das abenteuerliche Herz: Aufzeichnungen bei Tag und Nacht. Berlin: Frundsberg-Verlag, 1929.

Die totale Mobilmachung. Berlin: Verlag für Zeitkritik, 1931.

Der Arbeiter: Herrschaft und Gestalt, Hamburg: Hanseatische Verlagsanstalt, 1932.

Blätter und Steine. Hamburg: Hanseatische Verlagsanstalt, 1934.

Afrikanische Spiele. Hamburg: Hanseatische Verlagsanstalt, 1936.

Das abenteuerliche Herz: Figuren und Capriccios. Hamburg: Hanseatische Verlagsanstalt, 1938.

Auf den Marmorklippen. Hamburg: Hanseatische Verlagsanstalt, 1939.

Gärten und Strassen: Aus den Tagebüchern von 1939 und 1940. Berlin: Mittler, 1942.

Myrdun, Briefe aus Norwegen. Oslo, 1943 (special edition for the German armed forces).

Der Friede: Ein Wort an die Jugend Europas und an die Jugend der Welt. Amsterdam: Erasmus, 1946.

Atlantische Fahrt. London, 1947 (special edition for the German prisoners of war in England).

Sprache und Körperbau. Zürich: Die Arche, 1947.

Ein Inselfrühling; Ein Tagebuch aus Rhodos: Mit den sizilianischen

Tagebuchblättern "Aus der Goldenen Muschel." Zürich: Die Arche, 1948.
Strahlungen. Tübingen: Heliopolis-Verlag, 1949.
Heliopolis: Rückblick auf eine Stadt. Tübingen: Heliopolis-Verlag, 1949.
Über die Linie. Frankfurt a. M. : Klostermann, 1950.
Haus der Briefe. Olten: Vereinigung Oltner Bücherfreunde, 1951.
Der Waldgang. Frankfurt a. M. : Klostermann, 1951.
Am Kieselstrand. Frankfurt a. M. : Klostermann, 1951.
Besuch auf Godenholm. Frankfurt a. M. : Klostermann, 1952.
Drei Kiesel. Frankfurt a. M. : Klostermann, 1952.
Der gordische Knoten. Frankfurt a. M. : Klostermann, 1953.
Das Sanduhrbuch. Frankfurt a. M. : Klostermann, 1954.
Am Sarazenenturm. Frankfurt a. M. : Klostermann, 1955.
Rivarol. Frankfurt a. M. : Klostermann, 1956.
Serpentara. Zürich: Bösch-Presse, 1957.
San Pietro. Olten: Vereinigung Oltner Bücherfreunde, 1957.
Gläserne Bienen. Stuttgart: Klett, 1957.
Jahre der Okkupation. Stuttgart: Klett, 1958.
Mantrana: Einladung zu einem Spiel. Stuttgart: Klett, 1958.
An der Zeitmauer. Stuttgart: Klett, 1959.
Ein Vormittag auf Antibes. Olten: Vereinigung Oltner Bücherfreunde, 1960.
Sgraffiti. Stuttgart: Klett, 1960.
Der Weltstaat: Organismus und Organisation. Stuttgart: Klett, 1960.
Das spanische Mondhorn. Olten: Vereinigung Oltner Bücherfreunde, 1962.
Fassungen. München: Gotteswinter, 1963.
Typus-Name-Gestalt. Stuttgart: Klett, 1963.
Sturm. Olten: Oltner Liebhaberdruck No. 1, 1963.
Grenzgänge. Olten: Oltner: Liebhaberdruck No. 6, 1965.
Im Granit. Olten: Oltner Liebhaberdruck No. 12, 1967.
Subtile Jagden. Stuttgart: Klett, 1967.
Zwei Inseln: Formosa, Ceylon. Olten: Matheson, 1968.
Federbälle. Biberach an der Riss: Dr. Karl Thomae, 1969.
Lettern und Ideogramme. Olten: Oltner Liebhaberdruck No. 21, 1970.
Ad Hoc. Stuttgart: Klett, 1970.
Annäherungen: Drogen und Rausch. Stuttgart: Klett, 1970.
Philemon und Baucis: Der Tod in der mythischen und in der technischen Welt. Stuttgart: Klett, 1972.
Die Zwille. Stuttgart: Klett, 1973.

2. Collected Works
    The collected works appeared under the title *Werke.* 10 vols. Stuttgart: Klett, 1960 - 1965. Vols. 1 - 4: *Tagebücher;* vols. 5 - 8: *Essays;* vols. 9 - 10: *Erzählende Schriften.*

Note: *Werke* do *not* include the large number of articles which, in the main, appeared in various journals between 1920 and 1932. The topics are diverse: military, political, literary, and entomological. Since they are of but special interest, they are not listed here. For complete bibliographical data, see Hans Peter Des Coudres, *op. cit.* The short novel *Sturm* is also excluded from the collected works.

3. Compilations
The list comprises the books Jünger compiled and edited.
Die Unvergessenen. Berlin and Leipzig: Andermann, 1928. E.J. contributed "Vorwort," "Caspar René Gregory," and "Nachwort."
Der Kampf um das Reich. Essen: Deutsche Vertriebsstelle "Rhein und Ruhr," 1929. E.J. contributed "Vorwort."
Luftfahrt ist not! Leipzig: Vaterländischer Buchvertrieb Thankmar Rudolph [1930]. E.J. contributed "Vorwort."
Krieg und Krieger. Berlin: Juncker und Dünnhaupt, 1930. E.J. contributed "Vorwort" and "Die totale Mobilmachung."
Das Antlitz des Weltkrieges, vol 1: *Fronterlebnisse deutscher Soldaten.* Berlin: Neufeld und Henius, 1930. E.J. contributed "Krieg und Lichtbild," "Strosstrupps," "Der letzte Akt," "Krieg und Technik," and "Das grosse Bild des Krieges."
Das Antlitz des Weltkrieges, vol. 3: *Hier spricht der Feind: Kriegserlebnisse unserer Gegner.* Berlin: Neufeld und Henius [1931]. E.J. contributed "Vorwort."

4. Translations
Only a few of Jünger's books have been translated into English:
The Storm of Steel [In Stahlgewittern]. London: Chatto and Windus, 1929.
Copse 125 [Das Wäldchen 125]. London: Chatto and Windus, 1930.
African Diversions [Afrikanische Spiele]. London: Lehmann, 1954.
On the Marble Cliffs [Auf den Marmorklippen]. London: Lehmann, 1947 Also: New York: New Directions, 1947; Penguin Books, 1970.
The Peace [Der Friede]. Hinsdale, Ill. : Regnery, 1948.
The Glass Bees [Gläserne Bienen]. New York: Noonday, 1960.

SECONDARY SOURCES

1. Books
ARNOLD, HEINZ LUDWIG. *Ernst Jünger.* Berlin: Steglitz, 1966.
BANINE. *Rencontres avec Ernst Jünger.* Paris: 1951.
BAUMER, FRANZ. *Ernst Jünger.* Berlin: Colloquium, 1967.
BECHER, HUBERT, S.J. *Ernst Jünger: Mensch und Werk.* Warendorf: Schnell, 1949.
BENSE, MAX. *Ptolemäer und Mauretanier oder die theologische Emigration der deutschen Literatur.* Cologne and Berlin: Kiepenheuer, 1950.

Böhme, Ulrich. *Fassungen bei Ernst Jünger*. Meisenheim am Glan: Anton Hain, 1972.

Brock, Erich. *Ernst Jünger und die Problematik der Gegenwart*. Basel: Schwabe, 1943

———. *Das Weltbild Ernst Jüngers: Darstellung und Deutung*. Zurich: Neihaus, 1945.

Decombis, Marcel. *Ernst Jünger: L'homme et l'oeuvre jusqu'en 1936*. Paris: Aubier, 1943.

Hilsbecher, Walter. *Ernst Jünger und die neue Theologie*. Frankfurt a. M.: privately printed 1949.

Huizinga, J. *Homo Ludens: Versuch einer Bestimmung des Spielelements in der Kultur*. Amsterdam: Akademische Verlagsarstalt, 1939.

Jünger, Friedrich Georg. *Die Spiele: Ein Schlüssel zu ihrer Bedeutung*. Frankfort: Vittorio Klostermann, 1953.

Kranz, Gisbert. *Ernst Jüngers symbolische Weltschau*. Düsseldorf: Schwann, 1968.

Loose, Gerhard. *Ernst Jünger: Gestalt und Werk*. Frankfurt a. M.: Klostermann, 1957.

Martin, Alfred von. *Der heroische Nihilismus und seine Überwindung: Ernst Jüngers Weg durch die Krise*. Krefeld: Scherpe, 1948.

Mohler, Armin, ed. *Die Schleife: Dokumente zum Weg von Ernst Jünger*. Zürich: Die Arche, 1955.

Müller, Wolf Dieter. *Ernst Jünger: Ein Leben im Umbruch der Zeit*. Berlin: Juncker und Dünnhaupt, 1934.

Müller-Schwefe, Hans-Rudolf. *Ernst Jünger*. Wuppertal-Barmen: 1951.

Nebel, Gerhard. *Ernst Jünger und das Schicksal des Menschen*. Wuppertal: Marées, 1948.

———. *Ernst Jünger: Abenteuer des Geistes*. Wuppertal: Marées, 1949.

Paetel, Karl O. *Ernst Jünger: Wandlungen eines deutschen Dichters und Patrioten*. New York: Krause, 1946.

———. *Ernst Jünger: Weg und Wirkung, Eine Einführung*. Stuttgart: Klett, 1948.

———. *Ernst Jünger in Selbstzeugnissen und Bilddokumenten*. Reinbek bei Hamburg: Rowohlt, 1962.

Rausch, Jürgen. *Ernst Jüngers Optik*. Stuttgart: 1951.

Schwarz, Hans Peter. *Der konservative Anarchist: Politik und Zeitkritik Ernst Jüngers*. Freiburg im Breisgau: Rombach, 1962.

Stern, J. P. *Ernst Jünger*. Cambridge, England: 1953.

2. Festschriften

Arnold, Heinz Ludwig, ed. *Wandlung und Wiederkehr*, Ernst Jünger zum 70. Geburtstag. Aachen: 1965. Contains fifteen contributions.

Farbige Säume Ernst Jünger zum 70. Geburtstag. Special edition of *Antaios*, vol. VI, nos. 5 and 6. Stuttgart, 1965. Contains twenty-nine contributions.

MOHLER, ARMIN, ed. *Freundschaftliche Begegnungen,* Festschrift für Ernst Jünger zum 60. Geburtstag. Frankfurt am Main: Klostermann, 1955. Contains twelve contributions.

3. Polemics
BINGEL, HORST, ed. "Ernst Jünger: Fakten." *Streit-Zeit-Schrift,* vol. 6. no. 2. Frankfurt am Main, 1968. Contains twenty-four contributions.

4. Articles
The number of articles dealing with Jünger and his work is vast. Hence only a representative selection is offered here. For the period up to 1953, see Karl O. Paetel, *Ernst Jünger: Eine Bibliographie* (Stuttgart: 1953).

AMÉRY, JEAN. "Totale Demobilisierung: Ernst Jünger." In *Karrieren und Köpfe: Bildnisse berühmter Zeitgenossen.* Zürich: 1955.

AUER, ANNEMARIE. "Nachträgliches zu einem Jubelfest: Ernst Jünger und die formierte Gesellschaft." *Weimarer Beiträge,* 1966, pp. 581 - 605.

BADEN, HANS J. "Ernst Jüngers christliches Zwischenspiel." In *Der verschwiegene Gott.* München: 1963, pp. 55 - 84.

BEIN, SIGFRIED. "Le Travailleur' d'Ernst Jünger: Type, nom, figure." In *Synthèses,* Jan.-Fév. 1966, pp. 674 - 675.

BERNHARD, HANS-JOACHIM. "Die apologetische Darstellung des imperialistischen Krieges im Werk Ernst Jüngers." *Weimarer Beiträge,* 1963, pp. 321 - 355.

BESSER, INGEBORG. "Ernst Jünger: Persönlichkeit und Werk." *Die Pforte,* 2 (1949 - 50), pp. 614 - 659.

BROCK, ERICH. "Ernst Jüngers Sprachphilosophie." *Die Tatwelt,* (1942), pp. 16 - 29.

CLAIR, LOUIS. "Ernst Jünger: From Nihilism to Tradition." *Partisan Review,* 14 (1947), pp. 453 - 465.

DVORAK, ROBERT. "Die Sprache Ernst Jüngers." *Deutsche Beiträge,* 3 (1949), pp. 158 - 168; 235 - 242.

ENGEL, MARCEL. "Im Morgenrot Herodots: Ernst Jünger und due Antike." *Antaios,* 6 (1965), pp. 473 - 487.

GRACQ, JULIEN. Symbolik bei Ernst Jünger." In *Entdeckungen.* Stuttgart: 1965, pp. 208 - 214.

GRUENTER, RAINER. "Formen des Dandyismus." *Euphorion,* 46 (1952), pp. 170 - 201.

GUDER, G. "Ernst Jünger." *German Life and Letters,* 2 (1948), pp. 62 - 71.

HAFKESBRINK, HANNA. "Ernst Jünger's Quest for a New Faith." *The Germanic Review,* 26 (1951), pp. 289 - 300.

HARICH, WOLFGANG. "Ernst Jünger und der Frieden." *Aufbau,* 2 (1946), pp. 556 - 570.

HEISELER, BERNT von. "Ernst Jünger." In *Ahnung und Aussage,* Gütersloh: 1952, pp. 264 - 278.

HILLIGEN, WOLFGANG. "Mass, Bild und Klang: Eine Studie zur Sprache Ernst Jüngers." *Die Sammlung*, 8 (1953), pp. 442 - 449.

HOFFMAN, FREDERICK J. "The Moment of Violence: Ernst Jünger and the Literary Problem of Fact." In *Essays in Criticism*. Oxford: 1960, pp. 405 - 421.

HOHENDAHL, PETER UWE. "The Text as Cypher: Ernst Jünger's Novel 'On the Marble Cliffs.' " *Yearbook of Comparative Criticism*, 1968, pp. 728 - 69.

JANCKE, OSKAR. "Versuch über die Sprache Ernst Jüngers." *Hamburger Akademische Rundschau*, 3 (1948), pp. 392 - 395.

JUST, KLAUS GÜNTHER. "Die Sprache Ernst Jüngers." *Anstösse*, 1961, pp. 11 - 20.

———. "Das Tagebuch als literarische Form." In *Übergänge*, Bern: 1966, pp. 25 - 41.

KAISER, HELMUT. *Mythos, Rausch und Reaktion: Der Weg Gottfried Benns und Ernst Jüngers*. Berlin: Aufbau, 1962.

LACHMANN, EDUARD. "Die Sprache der Marmorklippen: Ein Beitrag zu Ernst Jüngers Stil." *Wirkendes Wort*, 4 (1953 - 54), pp. 91 - 101.

LENZ, SIEGFRIED. "Der Schriftsteller und Philosoph Ernst Jünger." *Die Zeit*, 1962, no. 16, pp.   .

LOOSE, GERHARD. "Zur Entstehungsgeschichte von Ernst Jüngers Schrift 'Der Friede.' " *Modern Language Notes*, 74 (1959), pp. 51 - 58.

LÜTHY, H. "Rivarols Jünger oder Jüngers Rivarol." *Der Monat*, 9 (1956 - 57), pp. 56 - 70.

MAJUT, RUDOLF. "Der dichtungsgeschichtliche Standort von Ernst Jüngers 'Heliopolis.' " *Germanisch-romanische Monatsschrift*, 7 (1957), pp. 1 - 15.

MANN, GOLO. "Der stoische Jünger." *Der Monat*, 13 (1960), pp. 77 - 83.

MARCIC, RENÉ. "Ernst Jünger und der Weltstaat." *Forum*, 1965, pp. 60 - 66; 122 - 132.

MAYER, HANS. "Bemerkungen zu einer Maxime Ernst Jüngers." In *Festschrift Ernst Bloch zum 70. Geburtstag*. Ed. R.O. Gropp. Berlin: Aufbau, 1955, pp. 241-248.

MENDELSSOHN, PETER DE. "Über die Linie des geringsten Widerstandes: Versuch über Ernst Jünger." In *Der Geist der Despotie*. Berlin: 1953, pp. 173 - 235.

MONTESI, GOTTHARD. "Die Ausflucht nach Heliopolis: Zu Ernst Jüngers Evangelium des Geistes." *Wort und Wahrheit*, 5 (1950), pp. 31-45.

MUCKERMANN, FRIEDRICH. S.J. "An Ernst Jünger: Zu seinem Buch 'Der Arbeiter.'" *Der Gral*, 27 (1932), pp. 81 - 86.

NIEKISCH, ERNST "Der Arbeiter." *Widerstand*, 7 (1932), pp. 307 - 311.

———. "Die Gestalt des Arbeiters." *Antaios*, 6 (1965), pp. 493 - 498.

PEPPARD, MURRAY B. "Ernst Jünger's 'Heliopolis.' " *Symposion*, 7 (1953), pp. 250 - 261.

———. "North Myths and Nihilism." *Monatshefte*, 46 (1954), pp. 1 - 10.

PINETTE, GASPARD. "Ernst Jünger in France." *Renascence*, 13 (1961), pp. 180 - 186.

PLARD, HENRI. "La tentation du détachment dans l'oeuvre d'Ernst Jünger." *Revue des Langues Vivantes*, 20 (1954), pp. 45 - 48.

————. "Ernst Jüngers Antwort auf die Krise der Gegenwart." *Universitas*, 13 (1957), pp. 1141 - 1147; 1279 - 1286.

————. "Sur l'évolution récente d'Ernst Jünger." *Études Germaniques*, 16 (1961), pp. 108 - 128.

PONGS, HERMANN. "Der Logos im Kampf mit dem Kollektiv: Ernst Jünger." In *Im Umbruch der Zeit*. Göttingen: 1952, pp. 175 - 205.

RAUSCH, JÜRGEN. "Ernst Jünger oder die Qual des Bewusstseins." In *Der Mensch als Märtyrer*. 1957, pp. 201 - 223.

RILLA, PAUL. "Der Fall Jünger." *Die Weltbühne*, 1946, pp. 76 - 80.

SCHMIELE, WALTER. "Vom Dandy zum Provokateur." In Horst Lehner (ed.), *Zeitalter des Fragments*. Herrenalb: 1965, pp. 57 - 76.

SCHROERS, ROLF. "Der kontemplative Aktivist: Versuch über Ernst Jünger." *Merkur*, 29 (1965), pp. 211-225.

SHAW, MICHAEL. "Ernst Jüngers Vorstellung von einer Intelligenz der Materie." *Zschr. f. deutsche Philologie*, 83 (1964), pp. 219 - 227.

————. "The Continuity of Ernst Jünger." *Univ. of Texas Studies in Literature and Language*, Austin, 6 (1965), pp. 472 - 485.

SOMBART, NIKOLAUS. "Patriotische Betrachtungen über die geistesgeschichtliche Bedeutung von Ernst Jüngers 'Arbeiter.' " *Frankfurter Hefte*, 3 (1965), pp. 390 - 400.

STÄHLIN, FRIEDRICH. "Ernst Jünger und Novalis oder die Wirklichkeit der Träume." *Muttersprache*, 1949, pp. 103 - 119.

STAVE, JOACHIM. "Mythos oder Form: Bemerkungen zu Ernst Jüngers Buch 'Auf den Marmorklippen.' " *Die Sammlung*, 1948, pp. 269 - 280.

STEIN, GOTTFRIED. "Ernst Jünger." *Frankfurter Hefte*, 3 (1948), pp. 443 - 454.

STIRK, S.D. "Ernst Juenger and the Peace." *Queens Quarterly*, 54 (1947), pp. 147 - 157.

USINGER, FRITZ. "Abenteuer und Geschichte: Zu Ernst Jünger's 'Strahlungen.' " *Die Neue Rundschau*, 61 (1950), pp. 248 - 266.

VIATOR, PAUL. "Ernst Jünger und der Nihilismus." *Wort und Wahrheit*, 1 (1947), pp. 295 - 312.

WINKLER, EUGEN GOTTLOB. "Ernst Jünger und das Unheil des Denkens." In *Gestalten und Probleme*, Leipzig: 1937, pp. 94 - 132.

WOODLAND, T.W. "Ernst Jünger's War Diaries." *German Life and Letters*, 8 (1954), pp. 298 - 302.

Index

(The works of Jünger, which have been cited, are listed under his name)